SOLOMON

Solomon

The Lure of Wisdom

STEVEN WEITZMAN

Yale

UNIVERSITY

PRESS

New Haven and London

Yale University Press books may be purchased in quantity for
educational, business, or promotional use. For information,
please e-mail sales.press@yale.edu (U.S. office)
or sales@yaleup.co.uk (U.K. office).

Frontispiece: Scenes from the life of Solomon as illustrated on the opening
page of the Song of Songs in a fourteenth century Jewish prayer book
from southern Germany. (David Kaufmann collection in the Library
of the Hungarian Academy of Sciences; reproduced with permission
from the Library of the Hungarian Academy of Sciences)

Set in type by Vonda's Comp Services, Morley, Michigan
Printed in the United States of America by Sheridan Books, Ann Arbor, Michigan

Library of Congress Cataloging-in-Publication Data
Weitzman, Steven, 1965–
Solomon : the lure of wisdom / Steven Weitzman.
p.   cm.—(Jewish lives)
Includes bibliographical references and index.
ISBN 978-0-300-13718-7 (hardcover : alk. paper)
1. Solomon, King of Israel.   2. Jews—Kings and rulers—Biography.
3. Bible. O.T.—Biography.   I. Title.
BS580.S6W44 2011
222'.53092—dc22
[B]   2010044594

A catalogue record for this book is available from the British Library.

10 9 8 7 6 5 4 3 2 1

To Mira Wasserman,
with gratitude and love

CONTENTS

Preface, ix

Acknowledgments, xxvii

1. A Life in Letters, 1

2. A Lust for Knowledge, 16

3. Succession Struggles, 33

4. Solomonic Judgments, 51

5. Sacred Books, Satanic Verses, 69

6. The King of Kings, 83

7. Building Heaven on Earth, 98

8. Mining for Solomon's Gold, 113

9. Difficult Questions from a Dubious Queen, 133

10. A Thousand and One Sex Scandals, 149

11. Afterthoughts, 168

For Those Seeking to Know More, 183

Index, 193

ALTHOUGH THIS BIOGRAPHY of King Solomon is unquestionably "unauthorized," that doesn't mean it emulates the typical unauthorized biography about the powerful and famous—that is, an account that is written without the endorsement or cooperation of its subject and that usually contains at least a few juicy scandals. Granted, all these characteristics are certainly true here, as I doubt that King Solomon, were he alive today, would approve of what we are about to reveal about him, but I nevertheless mean something different by ascribing such a label to this particular biography. There are many "authoritative" accounts of the king's life, both pious versions canonized by religious tradition as well as secular ones endorsed by university professors. By referring to this biography as "unauthorized," I mean to say that it is different from both kinds of account in that it rejects both the certitudes of religious tradition as well as the intellectual confidence of secular scholarship, learning from both perspectives in many ways but ultimately aiming to go beyond them.

To set the stage for what follows, I would like to try to describe my method as a biographer of a biblical figure. "Method" isn't exactly the right way of describing my approach, but it is informed by certain kinds of evidence, certain questions, and a certain perspective that I want to try to explain. To do that, however, we need to go back and reconsider the earlier, more authoritative accounts of King Solomon against which this book is responding: what it is that they reveal about him; what their sources of information are; why we should not blithely accept what they claim; and what there is to learn beyond what they already tell us about the king's life.

The single most authoritative account of Solomon's life is, of course, the Bible, which actually includes two accounts— 1 Kings 1–11 and a more tedious retelling of its story in 1–2 Chronicles. Despite certain inconsistencies in these sources, Jews and Christians have long considered them to be an accurate portrayal of Solomon's life. They leave open many gaps in the king's life, not least of which is the insight that his wisdom supposedly taught him, but these could be filled in by turning to other biblical books attributed to Solomon—Proverbs, the Song of Songs, or the Song of Solomon, and the book of Ecclesiastes, all thought to bear on different aspects of his life and thought. But what is the source of the Bible's information? Did its authors have records going back to Solomon's time? Is any of its account based on eyewitness testimony?

For many readers, the authority of the biblical accounts runs even deeper than any firsthand information that a human observer could provide. While Jewish tradition ascribes some books of the Bible to human authors (early rabbis credited Jeremiah with writing the account of Solomon's life in 1 Kings and attributed Chronicles to Ezra and Nehemiah), it also holds that these authors were not merely recording their own impressions. They were writing as prophets, moved by divine inspiration, and so their writing had the same status as the word of God, which is why they were included in the Bible. When it comes to the books attributed to Solomon—Proverbs, the Song of Songs, and Ecclesiastes—some rabbis questioned whether their content was not better understood as the mere musings of Solomon himself, but the majority concluded that these works too were the product of prophetic inspiration, recording a knowledge beyond anything the king knew on his own. This belief, that the Bible records a divine account of Solomon's life and wisdom, makes it the most authoritative source of information conceivable. To challenge its testimony is to challenge God himself.

One reason my account of King Solomon's life is "unauthorized" is that it does not take the Bible's authority for granted or confine itself to what is written there. This is not because I do not respect the traditional beliefs of the hundreds of millions who regard the Bible as divine revelation, but because I am heir to another way of reading its contents, an intellectual tradition that is skeptical of any assertion of absolute authority, especially one rooted in divinely revealed knowledge. This approach to the Bible is often referred to as critical biblical scholarship not because it sees something to criticize about the Bible in the usual sense of that verb but because it calls for using independent judgment to determine the Bible's origins and meaning. Critical scholarship has come to question the traditional religious view of the Bible as the word of God, seeing its content as akin to the literatures of other ancient Near Eastern cultures, and thus open to challenge and critical examination like any other humanly authored text.

Critical biblical scholarship has been around for over three centuries, and while there is no one person who deserves the credit (or the blame, depending on your perspective) for this kind of interpretation, if we had to trace its origins to a single individual, it would be the seventeenth century philosopher Baruch de Spinoza (1632–1677). Spinoza, who is one of the most important founding figures of modern secularism, did not go so far as to reject the Bible as a record of divine revelation, but he did question what religious authorities, Christian and Jewish, said about it, using reasoned analysis to challenge their interpretive authority.

Spinoza's radical new approach to the Bible included a reassessment of Solomon himself. In contrast to earlier Jews and Christians who believed that Solomon's wisdom was divinely revealed and was therefore perfect and all-encompassing, Spinoza argued that the king did not know everything. While the king understood many things about the world, his wisdom was not supernatural according to Spinoza but born of reasoning, a faculty common to all humankind, and was thus subject to error, as Spinoza demonstrated by exposing a tiny but telling mistake that slipped into the design of Solomon's Temple. 1 Kings 7:23 describes an object in the Temple known as the "molten sea," a circular bronze tub said to have a circumference of thirty cubits and a diameter of ten cubits. Those measurements, Spinoza pointed out, betray a crude grasp of mathematics for a sage supposedly endowed with perfect knowledge, for the circumference of a circle is not three times the length of its diameter (thirty cubits to ten) but slightly more—3.14 times the length, the ratio known as pi. Spinoza wasn't trying to make the king look stupid—Solomon was his favorite biblical figure, a fellow philosopher!—but if his wisdom was truly divine, he would not have been capable of such a miscalculation, however infinitesimal it might seem to us.

If this is true even of the wisest man in the world, how much more true must it be of those who claim to know what the Bible really means, though they might claim divine wisdom themselves. Earlier interpreters professed to be able to explain Solomon's apparent mistake. An example from Jewish tradition is a text known as *Mishnat Ha-Middot*, the earliest known work of Hebrew geometry attributed (probably falsely) to an ancient rabbi named Nehemiah, which sought to redeem Solomon's mathematical knowledge by claiming that his measurement of the tub's circumference was based on the basin's inner rim while its measurement of the diameter ran from one outer rim to the other—hence yielding a ratio different from what one would expect. Spinoza dismissed such solutions as fabrication—the text says nothing of how the tub was measured. In his view, traditional interpreters pretended to a wisdom that they did not really possess, coming up with explanations that had no real empirical basis in the biblical text and thus obscuring what was—and was not—possible to learn about it.

Spinoza may seem to be focusing here on a trivial detail, but he does so to make a larger point: Whatever eternal truths the Bible might convey have been filtered through the minds of fallible human authors like Solomon—authors who might be pious and wise but who were prone to mistakes and misjudgments because they understood the world from within the constraints of the human mind. It is for the same basic reason that Spinoza challenged the traditional religious understanding of the Bible, however authoritative it might seem. No interpreter can know more than what the senses and reasoned inference can reveal, and since so much of the Bible is simply unknowable—the grammar of biblical Hebrew is only partially understood, the biblical text is imperfectly preserved, and the circumstances of the Bible's composition are completely unknown—no mere human being can credibly claim to fully understand the Bible, to know what truths lie concealed between its lines. This might not seem like a radical claim today, but Spinoza advanced this argument in an age in which the religious establishment staked its authority on its supposed knowledge of what the Bible really means, and his critique was a questioning of its dominance. In fact, the reason that he

called his work a *Theological-Political Treatise* was that the issue
at stake in it was not just how the Bible ought to be interpreted
but the political consequences of that interpretation, and Spinoza's challenge to the intellectual authority of biblical interpreters was really an argument for limiting the political authority of religion.

Spinoza's ideas were not accepted in his own lifetime. He
himself was excommunicated by the Jewish community of Amsterdam and condemned by many as an atheist, and his writings
were considered scandalous long after his death. Eventually,
however, the perspective he introduced began to exert an influence on people in ways that our culture is still grappling
with. Under its influence, scholars began to doubt what they
thought they knew about the Bible, and this led them to develop new conceptions of how and why it was written that were
at odds with traditional understanding. This is relevant for our
purposes in that it has undermined the authority of biblical
books like 1–2 Kings and 1–2 Chronicles. One of Spinoza's
greatest contributions to biblical scholarship was simply to
point out that we do not know much about the history of biblical books like Kings. When were they written, by whom, and
for what reason? Spinoza developed some preliminary answers
to these questions, but a more important contribution was
simply raising them, and, for the more than three centuries
since he did, secular biblical scholars have been struggling to
answer them by using the sorts of evidence and methods that
scholars used to interpret and contextualize other ancient texts.
Critical biblical scholars have learned a lot about the biblical
text in this way, but in the process they have rendered it much
more difficult to rely on for Solomon's story than was the case
in premodern times.

One thing that scholars have learned about the Bible, for
example, is that we don't really know what exactly it consisted
of in ancient times. The Hebrew Bible read by Jews today is

based on a version known as the Masoretic text which is also the basis of many English translations, but it is only one of several ancient versions of the biblical text. Other versions include the ancient Greek translation known as the Septuagint and various biblical manuscripts found among the Dead Sea Scrolls, which are Hebrew texts like the Masoretic text but which often substantially differ from it. One of the goals of secular biblical scholarship, a project known as text-criticism, is to try to reconstruct from these different versions the content of the original biblical text before it was altered by changes introduced over the course of its transmission. That goal has proven elusive, however, and what text-critics have found instead is that there is no such thing as an original biblical text. It is fluid as far back as we can trace it.

A small but instructive illustration of what this can mean for our understanding of Solomon involves the most familiar story told of the king, the account of how he judged between two women vying for the same baby. Most of us can describe what happens in this episode whether or not we have ever read the biblical account in 1 Kings 3: the two women plead their case, the sword is suspended over the child, and then Solomon grants the baby a last-minute reprieve, resolving the case as he determines the identity of the true mother. But a tragic loose end is usually forgotten as the story is remembered today, that being the second child, who was accidentally smothered by its mother and scarcely acknowledged after its death. This child is largely forgotten partly because our understanding of the story is based on the particular version of the biblical text, the Masoretic Bible. The dead child has more of a presence in other ancient versions of the biblical text, however, such as the Septuagint, where, in a small deviation from the Masoretic text, Solomon orders both the dead child and the living one cut in two, with half of each to be distributed to each woman. This is the version of events that the first century historian Josephus knew, and its influence in the Christian world helps to explain why—in contrast to contemporary depictions of Solomon's judgment that follow the Masoretic text by picturing only the living child—so many Renaissance paintings of the episode (Raphael, Claeissens, Poussin) place both children before the wise king, living and dead.

Should this small detail in the Greek text be factored into our understanding of Solomon and his wisdom? The reminder of the dead child does affect our impression of Solomon in potentially important ways. It was hard-hearted enough to subject the real mother to the prospect of seeing her child murdered—and we will see that there were early Jewish interpreters who strongly objected to this and other aspects of Solomon's judicial method—but a feigned threat could perhaps be justified as the only way to establish the truth. Threatening to mutilate the dead child as well is a different matter, inflicting unnecessary torment on the other mother, a bereaved woman, after all, who may be acting as she does because she is in denial. Perhaps the addition doesn't make her look any more sympathetic, but it does change our perception of Solomon ever so slightly, making him appear a little crueler, a little more grotesque in his insistence on an equitable solution, and reminding us that his judgment isn't fully restorative, that there is an injustice, the death of an innocent child, that even he cannot remedy.

Such discrepancies between the different versions of the Bible may seem trivial when viewed as isolated examples, but they add up in ways that make the overall story of Solomon's life far more difficult to pin down than one would think given the familiarity of this story. Factual statements and even whole plot developments that appear in the Greek version aren't in the Hebrew, or are in the Hebrew of 1 Kings but have been deleted from Chronicles (or vice versa), and it is not always clear what is original and what is the later emendation. We tend to think of the Bible as an unchanging document, but scholars have discovered that there really is no such thing as *the* Bible, only snapshots of it at various points in history, as understood by different religious communities. This holds true for the story of Solomon, and consequently it is impossible for us to recount as if there isn't more than one way to do so.

But doesn't secular biblical scholarship also offer a way to judge between the different accounts of Solomon's life? Isn't there a truth that lies behind these different accounts, a flesh-and-blood Solomon, that we can know in the way we do other historical figures? And although we don't have the kinds of diaries, letters, and other literary sources that we do for modern figures like Einstein or Freud, does not archaeology, the study of the physical traces that past people have left of their lives, make it possible to bypass the questions one might have about the Bible and determine what the real king was like, how he actually lived?

In the mid-nineteenth century biblical scholars did indeed begin to use the then new field of archaeology to help them determine the truth of what really happened in biblical history, and Solomon was an especially promising subject because he is supposed to have built so much—palaces, walled cities, stables, and other enduring structures that an archaeologist might hope to find. But here too, as with the quest to reconstruct an original form of the biblical story, scholarly investigation has not brought us any closer to King Solomon; to the contrary, it seems to have made him more obscure and inaccessible.

It wasn't supposed to turn out this way. Until just a few decades ago, it seemed that biblical archaeologists had found precisely what they were looking for, uncovering a number of remarkable finds that seemed to corroborate the existence of a Solomonic kingdom in the tenth century B.C.E.: the stables in which he kept his horses in the ancient city of Megiddo; the mines from which he extracted his wealth; the port from which his fleet of ships would sail. These and other discoveries not only seemed to confirm that there was a Solomon, they indicated that his reign was an era of dramatic transformation for ancient Israel, securing it from attack, fostering the transformation of an agrarian people into a urbanized one, constructing monumental edifices that reflected a high level of organization and craftsmanship, developing the land's natural resources, and promoting vigorous diplomacy, trade, and other kinds of international exchange.

But that was the picture of Solomon's kingdom as it was reconstructed a few decades ago. Since then the archaeology has led biblical scholarship in a very different direction, not toward Solomon but away from him. All of the discoveries attributed to Solomon—the stables at Megiddo, the Solomonic copper mines at Timna, the Solomonic port of Ezion-Geber, Solomonic walls built around Hazor and other important cities—have been reexamined and reinterpreted, and all have been shown to belong to other periods. As recently as the 1970s, many scholars assumed on the basis of what they thought was the archaeological evidence that Solomon's reign was a real historical age, the earliest demonstrable period of ancient Israelite history, in fact, but that sense of clarity has broken down. Today, when not one single find can still be confidently attributed to the Solomonic era, it is no longer clear that there even was such an era.

Not even Solomon's greatest accomplishment, the Temple in Jerusalem, has been corroborated archaeologically. I know of only one attempt to find Solomon's Temple—not Herod's Temple from the Roman period but the First Temple, which supposedly lies somewhere underneath it—an excavation undertaken in 1911–12 by an Englishman named Montagu Parker, and it was a complete fiasco. Parker cast himself as a cutting-edge archaeologist, but he was actually an unscrupulous opportunist, seeking what he thought was an immense treasure buried in the Temple, and while he enlisted the help of a respected archaeologist, his staff also included an Irish clair-voyant to help direct his search. Initially he searched in the tunnels beneath the Temple Mount, which had only recently been uncovered, and made some important discoveries, but when he failed to find what he was looking for, and having promised a staggering return to his investors, he grew desper-ate and decided to break into the Dome of the Rock itself, one of Islam's most sacred and inviolable sites, hoping to find un-derneath it a legendary cave where a great treasure supposedly lay hidden. He did not discover treasure there either, but he was himself discovered by a guard who immediately began sounding the alarm, and the word soon spread that foreigners were trying to steal Solomon's ring and other sacred relics. Parker never found Solomon's treasure, or any evidence of his temple for that matter, but he did manage to spark what has been described as the first Palestinian national uprising.

In more recent times, a small vestige of Solomon's Temple did surface in the antiquities market, a small thumb-sized ivory ornament inscribed with the words "House of the Lord." For several years it was on display in the Israel Museum in Jerusa-lem as the only surviving relic of Solomon's Temple, not from the time of Solomon himself but as witness to the Temple that he built, but it too has recently been exposed as a con. The mu-seum, which paid $550,000 for the ornament, has since with-drawn it from display, and the suspected culprits are now on trial. Though the outcome is unclear as I write this, an acquit-tal does not validate the relic, which is clearly a forgery, and without it, there is at present no evidence at all of Solomon's Temple.

What the quest for Solomon's Temple has revealed in the end, if anything, is a profound gullibility in the field that, iron-ically, is rooted in a scientific need for evidence. This need to verify things, to have empirical evidence that one can see with one's own eyes, has proven so potent that it sometimes overcomes the caution and even the ethics that are supposed to constrain scholarship.

In the absence of any certain evidence for Solomon and his kingdom, the issue that scholarship is wrestling with today is what this absence of evidence means. Many continue to believe that the evidence is still out there to be found—scholars simply haven't looked in the right places, but if they keep trying, the truth may be just a few feet away. It is not an unreasonable position. We know of earlier periods of Jerusalem's history that have not left an archaeological imprint but that are attested in literary sources, and it is thus perfectly possible that something similar is true of Solomon's Jerusalem. And in fact, there is an archaeologist working in Jerusalem today, Eilat Mazar—the granddaughter of one of Israel's most important archaeologists, Benjamin Mazar—who claims to be making discoveries just outside the present-day "old" city of Jerusalem that confirm the kingdom of David and Solomon, including a large stone building she identifies as a palace of David mentioned in 2 Samuel 5:11 and a wall that she identifies with one built by Solomon according to Kings.

Others interpret the absence of evidence rather differently, however—and not just Palestinian archaeologists seeking to discredit the Jewish claim to Jerusalem, but also prominent Israeli scholars like Israel Finkelstein of Tel Aviv University, co-director of the current excavations at Megiddo. Finkelstein and others point out that much of the archaeological evidence has been misinterpreted by scholars willing to stretch the evidence to fit the biblical account, and he includes among this group scholars like Mazar, who uses methodology Finkelstein deems questionable. (Mazar tends to announce discoveries through press releases rather than in conference or peer-reviewed papers—circumstances that make it difficult to scrutinize her methodology—and she relies heavily on the biblical account to interpret her finds, which is rather circular reasoning because she is also relying on those finds to interpret the Bible.) But he goes further, declaring that the failure to find any trace of Solomon's kingdom after decades of searching does not mean that scholars haven't been trying hard enough; rather, it is a sign that Solomon never existed or at least that the biblical account of his kingdom is greatly exaggerated. There is evidence to support a different understanding of Israelite history, he argues—one in which Jerusalem does not emerge as a major royal center until two centuries after Solomon's time, and one where Solomon himself, if such a figure existed, was little more than a tribal chief, with a small kingdom, if we can call it that, of a few dozen small towns and villages.

Whatever the ultimate resolution of this debate, the bottom line is that, after more than a century of textual and archaeological investigation, we know virtually nothing about the historical Solomon. There are many reasons to doubt what I Kings and Chronicles report about King Solomon, but we do not know enough to reject his existence altogether, and consequently scholars are forced into precisely the position we dislike the most: admitting that we don't know one way or the other. Not even the most rudimentary biographical facts are known. We often date Solomon's reign to between 960 and 920 B.C.E. or thereabouts, but that is just an educated guess; since Solomon is not mentioned in any ancient Near Eastern source outside the Bible, we cannot be certain of when his reign fits in with other known historical events, and the chronological information to be found in the Bible itself is incomplete and often rather suspect. How can one develop a basic chronology, much less a full-fledged biography, out of so much uncertainty? How, then, could any credible scholar undertake to write a biography of Solomon? What could such a scholar possibly claim to know, and what could a book possibly reveal? I wrestled with these questions for a long time, and my inability to resolve them nearly kept me from writing this book. It irritates me when fellow scholars claim to know things that are not really knowable, and I felt that I myself would have to do exactly that to produce a biography of Solomon. But there was something about his story that would not release me—indeed something that spoke directly to the very problem I was struggling with in trying to write a biography of the king. Once I figured out what it was about Solomon's story that was keeping me enthralled, I realized that there may yet be a way to recover something real in it—not insight into the historical figure by that name but an understanding of why this story is still told thousands of years after its composition, what it evokes, why it resonates.

Part of what was drawing me into Solomon's story, I realized, was the way that it acted out a personal fantasy of mine: what it would be like to know everything, to be able to answer all the questions that I have, no matter how elusive or complicated their answer. God gives Solomon access to all life's secrets, and there is nothing he does not understand or cannot figure out. For me, as someone so intensely curious about the world that I have devoted my life to trying to answer the questions that I have about it, that makes Solomon more than just an admirable figure; he is a deeply enviable one, and I know I am not alone in this envy. Over the course of history, many scholars, scientists, and explorers have looked to Solomon as a precedent for what they themselves were striving to achieve through their investigations. The story of Solomon—as much as, perhaps more than, that of Prometheus, Socrates, and other fabled seekers of wisdom from classical lore—establishes the tantalizing prospect of perfect intellectual mastery and absolute certitude, of *fully* satisfying one's curiosity about the world.

But that wasn't the only thing that was connecting me to Solomon; there was also the way his story ends, the strange and disturbing twist that he takes in his final years. Despite everything he knows, Solomon ends his days as a fool. His wives lead his heart astray, and he begins worshiping false gods that he should have recognized as illusory. Knowing everything takes Solomon nowhere in the end, and if he reaches any kind of ultimate conclusion, it is only that his quest for wisdom and understanding was all a kind of delusion; he really understood nothing of value, life remained an impenetrable mystery, and even his desire for understanding was itself rooted in misunderstanding: "I set my heart to know wisdom and knowledge, and this turned out to be delusion and folly. I came to know that this too was a chasing after the wind" (Ecclesiastes 1:17).

For many earlier readers of the Bible, the end of Solomon's story demonstrated the futility of the quest for knowledge—if even the perfect wisdom of God himself did not help Solomon in the end, they reasoned, why should the rest of us, with our much more modest abilities, strive for understanding?—and that is precisely why I find his story so relevant even as I must also acknowledge its irretrievability, for I see my life as a quest for understanding, and it calls that quest into question. I thought I might learn something valuable by investigating the life of Solomon himself, but what I in fact discovered—that we are unable to get to the bottom of who Solomon really was or even to confirm his existence—only seems to confirm Ecclesiastes' claim that true understanding is impossible.

But as Ecclesiastes also notes, one can't really judge a life until one knows how it ends, and the end of Solomon's life, it turns out, is what motivated me to undertake this book despite the unknowability of its subject. The Bible itself says almost nothing about the king's final days, the period after his descent into folly, but early interpreters—Jews, Christians, and Muslims—filled in the gap. For many of them, the failure of Solomon's wisdom wasn't the end of his story—he was humbled by his failings and he realized that his wisdom wasn't really wisdom, but his quest for understanding continued in new if more chastened ways. Some even suggest that some time before his death he achieved some kind of ultimate understanding, not a new form of knowledge but a kind of post-wisdom wisdom accessible only to those who have given up on their ambition to know everything.

Spinoza would no doubt have dismissed these interpretations as another example of religious fancy, and so they are, and yet they resonate as true for me in another sense. What scholars thought they knew about Solomon has turned out to be illusory, but even in the wake of this failure, the king's example suggests, there are other kinds of insight that one might still seek—not the absolute, unassailable knowledge that earlier generations grasped for, but a more modest understanding that can emerge after a person realizes that ultimate wisdom is impossible.

This ultimate kind of understanding is what we are after in this biography, but by "ultimate" I do not mean an understanding that is complete or unassailably authoritative. If you are seeking a book that reveals definitive religious understanding, you will not find this one satisfying in any sense. It draws on a history of two thousand years of religious interpretation—Jewish, Christian, and Muslim—to help illumine the story, and finds much wisdom there, but it does not cede to such interpretation any special authority and sometimes uses the insights of traditional interpretation to make points that their authors did not intend. If you are hoping to resolve the debate over Solomon's existence, to get to the bottom of who he really was, this book will probably frustrate you, too; its narrative is informed by secular biblical scholarship, but that, as we have noted, can take us only so far, helping us to understand what we cannot know about Solomon but hardly ever allowing us to distinguish what is true from what is false in the biblical accounts. For those who want to learn more about either of these two approaches to Solomon—religious understandings of his story or efforts to illumine his history through secular scholarship—I have added some recommended readings at the end of the book, but my own account does not completely align itself with one approach or the other, disavowing any claim to a definitive understanding of the Bible in either a religious or a secular academic sense.

Who, then, is this book for, and what can it teach us about Solomon? It is for those who feel the Solomonic desire to know the secrets of life but who have come to suspect that those secrets may be unreachable. Such readers may be Jewish, Christian, or Muslim, and they may be religious or secular; the secrets that they are after may be encoded in a scriptural text, or perhaps they reject scripture as a source of truth and rely on secular modes of inquiry—history, philosophy, or science—to learn what secrets they can. What these readers share is not any particular religious background or level of commitment but rather a certain similarity to Solomon himself in the post-wisdom state that he is supposed to have reached at the end, sharing his sense that what seems like wisdom may not really be that wise, questioning even their own pretensions to wisdom but still open to a continued quest for understanding. I do not know how many readers of this sort will find this book, but if you happen to be among them, it is addressed especially to you.

What this book offers in lieu of an authoritative biographical account is a reading of Solomon's life as what the king himself might have described as a *mashal*, a parable, a story that has concealed within it a lesson or warning. Jewish legend has it that Solomon composed many such parables in his life—he was considered a master of the form—and perhaps it is not a coincidence that many of the parables that later rabbis would tell were often about powerful and wealthy rulers similar to Solomon. Such parables might describe how a king built a palace or took a journey, or his relationship to his family—the sort of life that Solomon led—but they are not actually about the king at all. He is but a symbol for God, and the other characters in the narrative—his wife and children, the counselors and servants—are symbols as well. It makes no difference for understanding the mashal that the king isn't real and that the events these stories describe never actually took place; the truth lies hidden behind the story, an insight or teaching encoded into the biographical form of a story about a king.

This version of Solomon's life is not a mashal in the traditional sense. Its king is a symbol not of God but of something very human, and I certainly do not want the reader to discount the surface content of my narrative, which in addition to telling the story of Solomon also aims to introduce the story of his story, how it has been reimagined over history. But in addition to these goals, I also intend this narrative as a kind of parable, an effort to illumine what it is that Solomon has come to symbolize in our culture—the desire to know, curiosity in its most intense form, the ambition to understand what the world seems to want to conceal. This desire has shaped our culture, both religious and secular; it is what motivates theologians, philosophers, and scientists to investigate the secrets of things, and its ambitions may prove our undoing. What I have come to realize is that this desire has a biography of its own, and it is this biography—where the wish for wisdom comes from, how it pursues its ambitions, the deals with the devil that it makes, and the tragic end that it often comes to—that is our true subject in this book, the parable encoded into the life of that master of parables, King Solomon.

ACKNOWLEDGMENTS

_____

I COVET SOLOMON'S WISDOM, but I do not envy the king his intellectual solitude. Solomon never needed advice. He thought alone, wrote alone, and judged alone, and as a result he didn't realize until very late in life that there are certain kinds of wisdom that can only be reached by relying on others for counsel and correction. I found myself often relying on others in such ways as I tried to trace the biography of Solomon's story—friends, respected colleagues, and a few students soon to be peers. Without meaning to suggest that they are responsible in any way for this book's shortcomings, it is a pleasure to acknowledge my indebtedness to them now: Shazhad Bashir, Mara Benjamin, Ra'anan Boustan, David Brakke, Shlomo Bunimovitz, Kathryn Dickason, Charles DiSimone, Lorenzo Di Tomasso, John Efron, Charlotte Fonrobert, Constance Furey, Kevin Gerson, Susan Gubar, Chaya Halberstam, Bert Harrill, Kevin Jaques, Richard Layton, Zvi Lederman,

Matthias Lehmann, Nancy Levene, Shaul Magid, William Newman, Aviva Orenstein, Ricardo Padron, Vered Shem Tov, Brad Storin, Stewart Vanning, Jeff Veidlinger, and Dror Wahrman.

I want to single out some people who played an especially important role in bringing this book to life. Anita Shapira and Steven Zipperstein, the outstanding scholars in charge of the *Jewish Lives* series, honored me with the opportunity to participate in their series; they are models not only of superb scholarship but of intellectual leadership and support. I feel honored as well to have the chance to work with Ileene Smith, editor-at-large for Yale University Press, and will always be grateful to her for being so open to how I wanted to write this book. I also want to acknowledge her assistant, Sarah Miller, for her patient guidance. At the end of the writing process, the text came into the hands of a very skillful manuscript editor, Jeffrey Schier, who helped me to navigate the considerable distance between my word processor and the readers I hope this book will reach.

Above all, I am grateful to my wife and intellectual partner, Mira Wasserman, to whom this book is dedicated. She is an exemplary rabbi with great intellect and heart, an incredible mother to our four children—Yosi, Hillel, Lev, and Or—and she has infused her love and wisdom into every page of this book, as she has done in every aspect of my life.

SOLOMON

1

A Life in Letters

IF THE FIRST IMPRESSION a person makes is based on physical appearance, then Solomon never really makes a first impression because the Bible doesn't tell us what he looked like. This is in marked contrast to all of Israel's previous kings. Saul is said to have been a handsome young man who stood head and shoulders above everyone else. David is described as good looking, ruddy, and having beautiful eyes. Even Solomon's older brothers merit physical description: no one was as beautiful as Absalom, with his striking long hair, and his younger brother Adonijah is also said to be handsome. Both looked the part of king even if they never got a chance to play it. But of Solomon's appearance the text says nothing, as if his appearance was completely unremarkable.

What the biblical text does tell us when it first introduces Solomon is how he got his name. It is always a signal that a biblical character is significant when the narrative pauses long enough to tell us where the character's name came from, and often that name tells us something significant about the role that this person is to play in Israel's history. Solomon's appearance might not tell us anything essential about his character— after all, the good looks of Saul, David, Absalom, and Adonijah only mislead the reader in the end, concealing something ugly in each of their characters. To know someone's name, on the other hand, is to know something fundamental about that person, to reveal a truth that mere appearance often conceals. This is certainly true of Solomon. The consonants from which his Hebrew name, *Shlomo*, is constructed—a mere three letters as it was written in the vowel-less biblical text, the Hebrew letters *shin*, *lamed*, and *mem*—contain within them the key to who he was, or at least who he was supposed to be.

But two issues make it difficult for us to unpack the significance of Solomon's name. To begin with, when we read the Bible in English translation, we encounter his name only indirectly, through the filter of another language, and we cannot see, for example, how the letters of his name keep recurring throughout the narrative of 1 Kings 1–11 in ways that seem meaningful. Beyond that linguistic impediment is our lack of skill in the art of deciphering names. In our culture, a name functions like a Social Security number: it differentiates us from other people; it labels us, but it does not disclose any information about who we really are. "A proper name is merely an unmeaning mark," observed the great philosopher John Stuart Mill. "Objects thus ticketed with proper names resemble . . . men and women in masks. We can distinguish them, but can conjecture nothing with respect to their real features." Assuming that names are arbitrarily assigned, that they are "unmeaning marks," we no longer expect them to reveal anything essential about the name-bearer and would not know how to decipher them if they did.

In the world described by the Hebrew Bible, however,

names work very differently: they convey meaning, they un-mask. As is true of Hebrew words in general, most biblical names comprise three consonants that carry their core mean-ing, and, according to the Bible, their combination—the way these letters come together in reference to special people or places—is no coincidence; it is a working out of the divine will. In biblical reality, a name is nothing less than a revelation. It can even foretell the future.

Solomon's own genealogy includes several telling examples. His family were distant descendants of Judah, one of Jacob's twelve sons, and the ancestor from which his kingdom, the kingdom of Judah, derived its name. Judah's name, "Yehuda" in Hebrew, derives from the word "praise," reflecting his mother Leah's gratitude to God: "She conceived again, bore a son and said, 'This time I will praise [*odeh*] the Lord'" (Genesis 29:35). Judah's name cannot be reduced to his mother's intentions, however. In ways that the cloudy-eyed Leah does not herself realize, the name she chooses for Judah also has a secondary, prophetic meaning that does not come into view until Jacob summons his twelve sons to his deathbed for a final blessing. It is only then, twenty chapters after Judah's birth, that the text discloses the hidden meaning encoded in Judah's name: "Judah, your brothers will praise you (*yoduka*). Your hand will be on the nape of your enemies; the sons of your father will bow down to you. A lion whelp is Judah; preying on others, my son, is how you will ascend. . . . He crouches and stretches out like a lion, and like a lion, who will provoke him? The scepter shall not de-part from Judah, nor the ruler's staff from between his feet" (Genesis 49:8–10).

In the reality that the Bible describes, the moment of death often brought with it a prophetic glimpse of the future, which the dying would try to convey to their heirs in their last words. Here Jacob is describing the destiny of Judah's descendants: Judah was not the first in line for anything—he was the fourth born—but despite his relatively lowly status, his descendants will go on to dominate Israel: they will vanquish all their enemies; the other tribes will submit to them; and in their midst a ruler who will reign in perpetuity will be established—an indirect reference to the dynasty that David establishes, a dynasty meant to rule forever. Jacob sees all this clearly only in the final moments of his life, but his play on Judah's name suggests that his future dominance had been determined long before, programmed into his identity at the moment of his birth.

The names of other figures in Solomon's lineage spell out their destiny in similar ways. Er, Judah's firstborn son, has a name that sounds like the Hebrew word for childlessness; sure enough, he dies before he can have a child. Mahlon, first husband of Solomon's Moabite great-great-grandmother Ruth, has a name that portends the illness (*mahlah*) that will kill him and set the stage for Ruth to marry Boaz, direct ancestor of David and Solomon. Not every name in the Hebrew Bible portends the future, but enough do that another member of Solomon's lineage, an obscure figure named Jabez, mentioned fleetingly in 1 Chronicles, tries to manipulate this strange linguistic principle to his advantage. The letters that constitute "Jabez" evoke the Hebrew word for pain or grief. Jabez's mother called him this because she bore him "in pain," but Jabez, grasping how biblical names worked, discerned that there must be a hidden reason for it, that his life was destined to be defined by pain, and so he prayed to God to protect him from "hurt and harm," hoping that it was possible to elude the fate decreed by his name.

Solomon is heir to this tradition, but does he himself continue it? Is his destiny—as ruler, as temple-builder, as sage—also encoded in his name? In the story of Solomon's naming, the biblical text offers no indication of any portentous meaning: "David comforted Bathsheba his wife and went to her, and lay with her; and she bore a son, giving him the name Solomon" (2 Samuel 12: 24). What is missing from this scene are many of the motifs that characterize the most famous birth stories of the Bible and that indicate a special destiny for the child. No angel visits the parents before the woman conceives, and no prayer or miracle helps to bring the birth about. To the contrary, Solomon's birth is preceded by the opposite of a miracle, the death of an infant brother Solomon will never know, struck down by God to punish King David for his adulterous affair with Bathsheba. In keeping with the nondescript character of Solomon's birth, and in contrast to the births of so many of his ancestors, the text does not suggest any meaning for his name, much less one that portends his destiny.

This hasn't stopped scholars from trying to come up with such a meaning. The theory to which I am most sympathetic takes its cue from the fact that David was trying to comfort Bathsheba for the death of their first child when Solomon was conceived. Solomon's name can be parsed as "his replacement," and the circumstances suggest that David saw in him a substitute for the child that he lost. It is a touching idea, but there are problems with it, not least of which is that it imputes to the king more grief, and more humanity, than he would seem capable of. "Now he is dead. Why should I fast?" asks David when asked why he was not mourning for the baby. "Can I bring him back again:? I shall go to him, but he will not return to me." David had proven himself a very demonstrative mourner in the past, but those acts of grief were arguably insincere, public relations acts performed to keep the ambitious young ruler on the good side of public opinion. When the loss is private— only David's servants are present to witness his response to the child's death—the king's emotional detachment comes to the surface. The child is gone; he cannot be brought back. To interpret the naming of Solomon as David's remembrance of a dead child does not fit with this stony-hearted resolve to move on.

Actually, it is not even clear that it was David who gave Solomon his name. A scribal tradition recorded in the Masoretic Bible has preserved an alternative form of the verse in which it is Bathsheba, not David, who names the child. This alternative reading could be the original one; it is certainly in line with many other biblical stories in which it is the mother who gives the child his name. But if Bathsheba is the one who gave Solomon his name, what might she have intended by it? Did she conceive of Solomon as a replacement for her first child? For Uriah? Or maybe there is a less sentimental motive at work. The letters that make up Solomon's name can also mean "pay back" or "exact revenge" (both replacement and revenge involve the making whole of a loss). Bathsheba, like so many of David's other wives, had suffered many losses at the hands of David—he had robbed her of her honor, her first husband, and her first child—and she thus had many reasons to seek revenge. Might she have seen in Solomon's birth an opportunity to get back at David, a chance to replace *him?* If so, the name she selects, Solomon, may be the first sign of a plot beginning to take shape.

The biblical text allows for these and any number of other backstories, but all rest on mere speculation, and they draw us away from what we know from other biblical birth stories: that names in ancient Israel do not merely reflect the parents' feelings, as they do in our own culture, but are prophecies of a preordained destiny that they cannot yet see. The only other thing we can tell from the one-verse account of Solomon's birth, after all, is that God has a special interest in this child. 2 Samuel 12 continues: "And he (or she) called him Solomon, and the Lord loved him, and he sent word by the hand of Nathan the prophet and he called his name Yedidyah for the sake of the Lord" (2 Samuel 12:24–25). God has clearly put some thought into what to call Solomon/Yedidyah, selecting a name that recalls David ("David" and "Yedidyah" derive from the same root), but what is most relevant is the way it anticipates Solomon's future, the fateful role of love in his life—the love of God, and the love of women. The question for us is whether God has packed similar prophetic significance into the name "Solomon."

Early interpreters of the Bible certainly believed that it had such significance. The first reader known to have sensed something prophetic about Solomon's name was the author of Chronicles, who lived sometime after the Babylonian exile. With its lengthy genealogies and detailed description of the Temple and its cult, Chronicles can put a contemporary reader to sleep, but in antiquity, this reworking of the stories of Samuel and Kings played the opposite role: the High Priest's deputies read it to him on the eve of the Day of Atonement to prevent him from falling asleep on the job. In its Greek and Latin translations, Chronicles is known as the *Paralipomenon*, or "the things that have been left out," because it fills in what its author believed was missing in the earlier biblical sources, and one of the gaps that it colors in is the hidden meaning of Solomon's name.

In the Chronicler's account, it is David who reveals this meaning. In 1 Chronicles 22, the king summons his son and charges him with building a house for the Lord, a temple in which Israel could worship God. The content of David's speech to Solomon is drawn primarily from a passage that appears in 2 Samuel 7, an oracle delivered to David by the prophet Nathan, but the Chronicler supplements Nathan's words in an effort to resolve unanswered questions. In 2 Samuel 7, for example, God refuses to allow David to build the Temple, but the text does not explain why, or why, for that matter, God would subsequently permit Solomon to play this role. Chronicles inserts an explanation into David's speech stating that God forbade him from building a temple because he had shed so much blood during his reign; it would take a man of peace to do so. The same speech in 2 Samuel 7 speaks of a future descendant of David who will go on to build the temple and establish a permanent dynasty, but it does not provide a name, and this heir could in theory have been any of David's sons. Chronicles resolves this ambiguity as well by having David explicitly name the descendant in question as Solomon: "A son will be born to you; he shall be a man of peace, I will give him rest from all his enemies that surround him, for his name shall be Solomon, and I will give peace (*shalom*) and quiet to Israel in his days" (1 Chronicles 22:9).

Long before Solomon was born, according to the Chronicler, God had revealed to David what his name would be, and that name, derived from the word for peace, did indeed foretell his future. As king of Israel, he would bring peace and quiet to his people, who had known nothing but warfare since their arrival in the land of Canaan. As a man of peace, he would also by implication be able to finish the temple that David was forbidden to build because of the blood that he had shed.

The Chronicler isn't quite making things up from scratch here. Buried in the original oracle in 2 Samuel 7 is a possible allusion to Solomon's name, hidden in the prediction "He will build a temple for my name." The key phrase is "for my name," actually a single word in Hebrew, *lishmi*, which, as someone with a knack for word puzzles might notice, is built of the same three consonants that constitute Solomon's name, only in a different order. Arguably, then, the Chronicler is merely making explicit what is implicit in 2 Samuel, but only arguably so. We cannot be certain that the author of 2 Samuel intended to refer to Solomon, and that ambiguity may be important to the story that 2 Samuel is trying to tell. For even if the oracle in 2 Samuel 7 does indeed hint at the name of God's chosen successor to David, the reader cannot at this point in the story guess that it refers to Solomon, for there is another, more likely possibility, another member of the household whose name incorporates the word "shalom."

The person in question is Solomon's older brother Absalom

—"Avshalom" in Hebrew—a beloved son of David, a prominent member of his court, and the most qualified candidate for the role of king. Absalom did have an older brother, Amnon, whom one might normally have expected to inherit the throne, but fate ruled him out for this role, or rather Absalom himself did when he slew Amnon for raping and dishonoring his sister Tamar. Despite his disapproval of Absalom's act, David can scarcely bring himself to punish his favorite son. Absalom is beautiful. He has charisma. He gains the favor of the people by promising to secure justice for them should he become king. He seems to have the makings of a great ruler. Solomon at this point hasn't even entered the picture, and when he does he hardly seems a likely candidate for the throne, not technically a bastard but born under suspicious circumstances shortly after David's adulterous affair with his mother. A reader who does not yet know how the whole story is going to end would have had every reason to believe that if the prophet was alluding to anyone specific through his pun on the word shalom, it was the heir apparent, Absalom.

This is not to suggest that Nathan actually did have Absalom in mind. We simply do not know what he really intended. What I am suggesting is that 2 Samuel merely means to raise this as a possibility, to leave open more than one option, and thus to create some doubt about what exactly God had in mind for the future. Like the Chronicler, the author of 2 Samuel believed in God's control over human history, but that control is not as complete as it is in Chronicles, or as easy to understand. Humans can fail to live up to their destined role; they can even deliberately change their destiny as David does by repenting after his sin with Bathsheba, and God can change course as well, amending his plans, even abandoning them. Prophets like Nathan know something of what God intends for the future, but even what they see is ambiguous and susceptible to revision. This difference is reflected in the two versions of Nathan's oracle. In the Chronicler's version, Solomon's reign, like Israel's history in general, follows a straightforward, completely comprehensible divine plan, the plan encoded into his name, and everything works out the way it was always intended. In Samuel, things are murkier. Maybe Solomon is destined to be David's successor; maybe it was Absalom who was meant for this role. We cannot tell for certain and perhaps we aren't meant to know at this point in the story, and this ambiguity, I am suggesting, is meaningful, reflecting the author's sense of history as opaque and open-ended despite God's control: we are given enough information to know that there is a divine plan, but we cannot be certain how exactly things are meant to play out, and whether what we think will happen is really going to turn out that way.

With time, of course, it becomes clear that Absalom isn't the son God had in mind—he eventually rebels against David and is slain in battle—but what of Solomon? How can we be certain that he is the one whom God had in mind? It is to address this question that the narrative at last activates the prophetic meaning concealed within his name, though it does so not proleptically as the Chronicler does but only in retrospect, after Solomon begins to realize his destiny. Here is where translation obscures an important part of the story. What the English version conceals is a series of puns planted throughout 1 Kings 1–11, words that draw on the same letters that compose Solomon's name and that are meant to signal that he is fulfilling the destiny that it anticipates.

First of all, there is the pun that the Chronicler makes explicit, the play on the word *shalom*, or "peace." During David's reign, the warfare had never stopped, for after he subdued the Philistines, David had to confront many other hostile neighbors—the Moabites, the Arameans, the Edomites, the Ammonites—and then found his kingdom consumed by civil war with Absalom and other rebels. Solomon is quickly able to establish peace on all his borders, and not through conquest so far as we can tell but through diplomacy—treaties, alliances, and trade. What is clear in the Hebrew that does not come through well in translation is how his peacemaking ties in to his name. "He had peace (*shalom*) on all sides around him," 1 Kings 5:4 reports, and the word appears again a few verses later, in 5:26: "There was peace (*shalom*) between Hiram and Solomon" (Hiram, the king of a neighboring Phoenician city, was one of Solomon's most important allies). What the pun on Solomon's name implies is that the king's peacemaking was a role he was meant to play from the beginning, as the Chronicler discerned.

And this is far from the only way in which the root of Solomon's name prefigures his life. *Shalom* does not merely convey the absence of war, it also conveys completion or wholeness, and that connotation anticipates another aspect of his life, Solomon's role as a completer, the one who finishes what his father had begun by building the temple that David had been unable to build. "Completed (*watishlam*) was all the work that the king Solomon had done" (1 Kings 7:51), the Bible reports after he builds the Temple, and in case you missed the pun the first time around, it finds a way to repeat the root not once but twice at the end of its account of the Temple's construction: "Solomon offered up burnt offering and well-being sacrifices (*shelamim*) three times a year on the altar that he built for the Lord . . . and he completed (*weshilem*) the Temple" (9:25). The more deeply one reads into the Hebrew text, in fact, the more one realizes that Solomon's name surfaces everywhere in his story. Its letters inhabit the name Jerusalem (*yerushalaym*), the capital of his kingdom and the site of the temple that he is to build; look closely enough and you can even find it hiding in the description of his wisdom, albeit scrambled into a different order: "He spoke three thousand *proverbs*" (*mashal*, the same word that the rabbis would later understand to mean "parable") (5:12).

Once one cracks the code, everything in Solomon's life takes on a different significance. On the surface, Solomon's ascension to the throne seems like a fluke, an accident of history that would not have happened had David and his other sons done what they were supposed to do. Were it not for his father's failings, Solomon never would have been born—his father's relationship with his mother was a prohibited one—and he certainly should not have become king; that honor should have gone to older brothers like Amnon and Absalom. But once one detects the uncanny relationship between Solomon's name and the course of his life, the truth comes into focus, if only retrospectively: everything that happens in Solomon's story—the sins and tragedies that lead to his birth, his peacemaking, his wisdom, the Temple—is hinted at in advance by the letters of his name.

But here is where we have to call to mind the difference between Chronicles and its sources, the way Samuel and Kings resist the reader's effort to understand God's plan by depicting history's unfolding as ambiguous, unpredictable, and surprising. The puns on Solomon's name lead us to think that everything is going according to plan, that Solomon's name did predict his future, but just as that future is on the verge of completion, something unexpected happens: Solomon marries foreign wives and begins to worship their gods, the deepest possible betrayal of God, and that will lead in turn to the dissolution of his kingdom and eventually, centuries later, to the destruction of the temple that he had built. This wasn't part of the script. Nathan had never made any reference to this twist, and God himself doesn't seem to have anticipated it. And as if to underscore how far things have strayed from how they were supposed to transpire, the narrative makes yet another pun on Solomon's name, recalling his destiny again but this time in a way that suggests the king's failure to live up to it: "In the time of Solomon's old age, his wives led his heart astray after other gods, and his heart was not full (*shalem*) with the Lord his God as the heart of David his father" (1 Kings 11:4). By this point in the story, we know that the presence of a word with the same root consonants as Solomon's name is never an accident, but here those letters are preceded by a *not*. It is as if the narrative is telling us that Solomon has stopped acting like Solomon.

Later in the same chapter, the narrative seconds this point through another clever pun on Solomon's name. To punish the king for his sins, God vowed to tear most of his kingdom from his control—not all of it; he would leave Judah under the control of Solomon's successors—but it would be reduced to a small rump of a state, and to implement this plan he turned to an overseer of Solomon's laborers, Jeroboam of the tribe of Ephraim, to lead a rebellion. To inform Jeroboam of his intentions, God sends a prophet to meet Jeroboam, a fellow named Ahijah of Shiloh, and—as Israelite prophets were wont to do— Ahijah used a prop to convey his prophecy in a dramatic form. The prophet had put on a new robe before meeting Jeroboam, and when the two were alone, he took hold of it and tore it into twelve pieces, offering ten to Jeroboam. What did the act mean? The robe symbolized Israel, and the prophet's gesture was his way of announcing that God was about to tear ten of the twelve tribes from Solomon and hand them over to Jeroboam to form a new kingdom.

The relevant point here is the Hebrew word for robe, *salmah*, another pun on Solomon's name. It is pronounced with an *s*, not a *sh*, but graphically the two words are almost identical in their original language. But here again, the narrative evokes Solomon's name only to nullify it. The prophet does not seem to have been thinking only in terms of visual effect when he chose the rending of a cloak to symbolize God's punishment; he also appears to have been thinking linguistically, choosing an object that calls to mind Solomon's name, and in turn, everything that name calls to mind—peace, completion, the

Temple, Jerusalem. To tear the cloak into pieces was thus not merely to dramatize the dissolution of Solomon's kingdom; it was to symbolize the end of Solomon himself, or of what Solomon was supposed to be, the promise embedded in his name.

In *The Golden Bough*, the great nineteenth century folklorist James Frazer describes as primitive a mentality that can not clearly discriminate between words and things, that believes one can know everything about a person—his character, his future—by knowing his name. The biblical attitude is similar—Solomon's name does seem to predict his life—but there is a difference. In the Bible, the link between words and the world is not inevitable. It can be broken; people can avoid the destiny decreed by their names, as Solomon's ancestor Jabez did by praying to God to escape the pain portended by his name, or, like Solomon, they can go astray, failing to live up to that destiny. A name still encapsulates who a person really is, but only potentially, provisionally, because the unscriptability of human behavior—people's tendency to stray from the roles they are supposed to play—can snap a name's link to reality, turning it into an "unmeaning mark," no longer a revelation of a person's destiny but a mask concealing something underneath.

From the moment that Solomon fails in this way, a schism emerges between who he was supposed to be and who he turned out to be. The destiny that Solomon was supposed to fulfill, the idealized son of David foreseen by the prophet Nathan in 2 Samuel 7, would survive in a way, but it would have to be attached to another son of David, the messiah, who (in Jewish tradition) has had various names attached to him, including the word "Peace" but none that has been tested against reality, as this figure has yet to appear. The Solomon of Kings, on the other hand, is a much more disappointing figure, a shadow of who he was meant to be, sinful, self-deluded, seeming to forget everything that his wisdom taught him. He would rule for a total of forty years, no mean accomplishment in an age when many kings died prematurely, but he never again accomplishes anything of note, and the author of Kings seems to lose interest in his story after the meeting between Jeroboam and Ahijah, skipping over the remainder of Solomon's reign as if from the moment that his life deviates from the destiny decreed by his name, there was nothing more worth saying about it except to register its end.

But from my perspective, as a reader of the biblical text, I cannot honestly say that I am disappointed that Solomon didn't live up to his name. To be sure, had he but stuck to the script, biblical history would have been far less catastrophic—his kingdom would never have been torn asunder, the Temple would never have been destroyed, the descendants of David and Solomon might still be ruling to this day as God originally promised—but one has to admit that this history would also be far less interesting as well. The Solomon of Kings caused much pain by deviating from the destiny he was born to play, but in the process he also became a much more complex and compelling figure—hard to pin down, inconsistent, open-ended—good news for the history of Jewish storytelling if not for the Jews themselves. This is the life we will be trying to understand from here on out—not the flawless, monotonous ruler of Chronicles who always lives up to the destiny decreed for him from his birth, but the more elusive, unpredictable, secretly flawed figure of Kings, the Solomon concealed rather than revealed by the letters of his name.

2

A Lust for Knowledge

IN OUR CULTURE, childhood is understood as a formative period. In the Bible, childhood barely registers as a significant part of a person's story. For a book read by so many children, it tells remarkably few stories about them other than the exception of a miraculous birth now and then, and when children do show up in its narratives, they are presented as scaled-down grown-ups, smaller, dependent on adult care, with less status, but with their essential traits and destiny already established.

The biblical story of King Solomon is no exception: the book of Kings says almost nothing about his upbringing, education, or earliest relationships. One of the few pieces of information that we can glean is that Solomon had many older brothers. According to Chronicles, six sons were born to David while he ruled from his base in the city of Hebron—Amnon, Daniel, Absalom, Adonijah, Shephatiah, and Ithream—and still other brothers born after he moved to Jerusalem, including a brother named Nathan who may or may not be the prophet that gave Solomon the name Yedidyah. But 2 Samuel and 1 Kings give us information about only a few of these brothers, and only those who threaten Solomon's future as king by vying for the throne themselves, and we are told nothing at all about any of the other people who may have populated his childhood—sisters, servants, friends, or teachers.

Despite the lack of evidence, however, a modern reader cannot help but think that something significant lurks in the gap that represents Solomon's childhood. We owe this presumption in large part to another Solomon, Sigmund Freud, who coincidentally inherited the Hebrew name *Shlomo* from his grandfather. Freud is relevant here because, of course, he is famous for his ability to recover lost childhood experience buried in the unconscious but retrievable through a method that Freud likened to that of archaeologists, "whose good fortune it is to bring to the light of day after their long burial the priceless though mutilated relics of antiquity" ("Fragment of an Analysis of a Case of Hysteria"). Even our own earliest childhood experiences are known to us only in a fragmentary way, much of them forgotten or never fully registered to begin with, but Freud developed a way to bring such experience back to the surface.

But how do we retrieve the memory of Solomon's childhood from a text that never mentions it? We cannot sit Solomon himself on a couch, and nothing in the text suggests there is something hidden about him either, no discernible indications of a repressed childhood. But Freud himself believed that the experiences of childhood were among the most durable elements of human experience, preserved intact because they were buried away in the unconscious just as ancient artifacts could be buried underground and preserved for thousands of years, whereas conscious experience was subject to a continuous process of wearing away. One only need know how to locate and bring these experiences to the surface, and this was where the techniques of psychoanalysis were of use, a kind of archaeology of the mind through which one could dig down through its sediments into the earliest periods of childhood.

Freud used such techniques to excavate the biblical text itself, employing them in *Moses and Monotheism* to retrieve the repressed childhood experience of Israel itself from the biblical narrative. The resulting biblical interpretation seems completely fanciful now—Freud surmised that the Exodus story suppresses the memory of Moses's murder by the Israelites—but more recent scholars, like the Jerusalem-based Aviva Zornberg, have gone on to refine his approach, detecting what Zornberg calls the "biblical unconscious": desires, conflict, trauma, and other mental processes never overtly described by the text but that have left traces of their presence. I have to admit that I am not completely persuaded by such analyses—as Zornberg herself all but acknowledges, they do not so much prove their case as seduce one into accepting them—but I can think of no other way to retrieve the unrecorded secrets of Solomon's childhood experience.

One might begin such an analysis by examining the family from which Solomon originated for evidence of how he was raised and his relationship to parents and siblings. The "House of David," as this family was known, was an unhappy one if there ever was one, its dysfunction greatly magnified by the number of David's wives and children. Some of those wives had reason to resent David—Michal, the daughter of Saul, probably suspected him of complicity in her father's death and certainly disliked the way her husband comported himself in public. But even apart from such personal grievances, Harems are often fiercely competitive places, and David's wives probably built up many mutual resentments as they jockeyed to position their sons to inherit the throne. The older wives probably had a special disliking for Bathsheba because her adulterous affair with David had brought shame on the family and also because of her rare beauty. The sons of such a woman were almost certainly looked down on too, allowed to remain in the household only because of their father's protection.

The dysfunction of Solomon's family erupted into full-scale conflict in his own generation. David loved his children, but he didn't intervene in their internal conflicts, which made them worse. Amnon started the trouble by luring his half-sister Tamar to his apartment, raping her, then further shaming her by casting her out. This infuriated Tamar's brother Absalom, who sought revenge by luring Amnon to his death, and that act then deepened the antagonism between Absalom and David himself. Absalom was a beautiful and charismatic leader, and he used his popularity with the people to stir up a rebellion against his father, adding sexual insult to injury by sleeping with the concubines that his father had left behind during his flight from Jerusalem. Absalom died in that battle, but his brother Adonijah seems to have inherited some of the same resentments and similar desires, making his own attempt to usurp the throne and, later, to sleep with one of David's female companions, a beautiful woman named Abishag. This was the household in which Solomon grew up, these were his closest kin and perhaps his role models, and one would expect such a disturbing legacy to have shaped his development.

But reconstructing this impact is all but impossible. The Bible simply doesn't tell us anything about the psychology of the young king Solomon. We don't know if he knew the scandalous events that preceded his birth or if he was aware that it was the death of his parents' first son, his unnamed older brother, that led to his own conception. We cannot determine his relationship to older brothers like Amnon and Absalom— they had a different mother and may have had little interaction with him. Later interpretive tradition supplies a number of intriguing stories about his relationship with Bathsheba, sometimes suggesting that the son distrusted his mother, but such episodes have no basis in 1 Kings. Its author shows no interest in Solomon's upbringing other than how he got his name and how he became king, leaving the rest of his childhood unremembered.

Since we have no other way of filling in this gap in Solomon's life, however, let us not give up on a Freudian approach so easily. From Freud and followers like Zornberg, one learns that while buried memory may not be registered on the surface of the narrative, it sometimes surfaces indirectly, in odd or haunting imagery, word choices, and turns of phrase that have bubbled up from the depths of the unconscious and express— fleetingly, enigmatically, but revealingly—the desires and anxieties hidden there. Rabbinic interpretation often seems to pick up on these clues, as if it were somehow intuitively tapped into the unconscious, and Zornberg draws on its insights to develop her own readings. Those are nearly impossible to imitate; her intuition and learning are almost uncanny. Without any other way into the lost childhood of Solomon, however, we have to do our best to follow her methodology.

As we have noted, 1 Kings does not describe Solomon's childhood, but, reading over its early chapters from this perspective, one finds there at least one indication to suggest a childhood marked by an active but hidden mental life. The first of these clues surfaces in David's final instructions to Solomon in 1 Kings 2:1–9, the only words of father to son recorded in the biblical text. This may not seem like much to go on, but here too Freud is an inspiration, for as it happens, we have but one direct record of what his father said to him, a Hebrew dedication inscribed into a childhood Bible. The inscription (which coincidentally happens to address Freud as Shlomo) is just a few lines, but, poring over its details, scholars have drawn a number of conclusions about Freud's relationship to his father, and thus there is hope for us that even a single, small relic of a father's love might be enough to reveal something about the young king's formation.

Not that there is much love expressed in David's last words to Solomon. As we noted briefly in our discussion of Jacob's last words in the previous chapter, the act of dying was seen by ancient Israelites as a moment of ultimate insight, of prophecy or wisdom at its most profound, and a number of biblical figures—Jacob, Moses, Samuel—use this moment to teach something important to their descendants, trying to get them to learn from the past or revealing to them their future. Not David: if anything, his last words to Solomon are distinguished by their lack of profundity. They begin in an encouraging way: "I am going the way of all the earth: be strong, be a man, keep the charge of the Lord your God to walk in his ways" (1 Kings 2:2), but such words are nothing more than a perfunctory and platitudinous preface to a series of instructions confirming that David is the conniving person his enemies always thought him to be. In contrast to Isaac, Jacob, and the other biblical figures whose last words are recorded, David's real purpose is not to teach or to bestow a blessing; it is the settling of scores with old foes. The reason he has summoned his son to his side is to give him a wish list of people to whack.

Critical scholarship has concluded that this speech isn't from David himself; it was written, or drastically rewritten, by an author living centuries after the king. If this view is correct, we can learn little if anything from it about Solomon's relationship to his father. But other readers, accepting it as authentic, have detected within it certain intimations of that relationship, and theirs is a more productive approach to the text for our purposes. Particularly significant from this perspective is the speech's references to Solomon's wisdom: "Act according to your wisdom," David urges his son in 1 Kings 2:6, and he refers to this characteristic again in 2:9: "You are a wise man." Although David's thoughts are focused on his own grievances, he does at least acknowledge Solomon's most outstanding trait—in fact, this is the only compliment he ever pays his son so far as we know. What is strange about this is that Solomon isn't supposed to be wise yet. God will not give him wisdom until the next chapter, in 1 Kings 3, but here is David referring to his son as if he was already well known for his wisdom.

Now it may well be that King David did not mean much by these references to Solomon's wisdom. By "act wisely," he may simply have intended "act prudently" or "act shrewdly," appealing to his son's sense of caution or opportunism rather than to some unusual level of insight. The word in Hebrew is the same word that the text will later use to describe Solomon's extraordinary understanding, however—*hokmah*—and that was enough for the early rabbis and other kinds of premodern interpreters to fill in the king's missing childhood. Since toddlerhood, they imagined, the young prince already exhibited the wisdom for which he would become famous, solving impossible court cases, answering difficult riddles, and composing proverbs. His father had been wise too, but even he was outsmarted by his son. The rabbis noticed certain slightly discrepant sentiments expressed in the book of Psalms (a record of David's thoughts) and the book of Proverbs (the teachings of Solomon), and these they attributed to Solomon's superior wisdom. Thus, according to one rabbinic interpretation, David is said to have made a pronouncement recorded in Psalm 111: 10—"the beginning of *wisdom* is the fear of the Lord"—only to find himself corrected by his son: "The fear of the Lord is the beginning of *knowledge*," cited in Proverbs 1:7. These statements seem to be saying the same thing, but the rabbis saw in their one-word difference a Solomonic challenge to David's authority, the precocious young prince presuming to improve on his father's wisdom.

I am not suggesting that we can use these stories to fill in the gap of Solomon's childhood in any direct sense. Apart from the fact that such stories are completely made up, they operate with a conception of childhood very different from the one posited by Freud. In contrast to Freud's method for reconstructing childhood, they do not work forward from childhood to understand the adult; they work backward from the adult to the child, using the traits of an adult Solomon to illumine the personality of his younger self. There is no need from this perspective to chart his psychological development because, from the moment the toddler prince can express himself, he is already formed.

What does strikes me about these stories, however, is their detection of something significant in David's words "Act according to your wisdom." Solomon's wisdom, we discover, has an unwritten history that precedes the wisdom he acquires in 1 Kings 3; the young Solomon's chief preoccupation, his most powerful desire from the very beginning, is his need to know. Later on, it will become clear that Solomon also needs wisdom for practical, political reasons—he needs understanding in order to govern the Israelites—but what we learn from David's last words is that Solomon's wisdom originated much earlier in his life, taking shape as his outstanding characteristic even before he became king. To understand the origins of this characteristic, we thus need to go back much earlier in Solomon's life.

But how to tease out this backstory? Again, we have to look for other relics of the unconscious past scattered in the text, and a particularly promising text is 1 Kings 3:5–14, which describes a dream Solomon has just after he becomes king. The dream occurs at an anxious moment in his life. He has just inherited the throne from his recently deceased father, and the young king is worried that he doesn't know enough to rule a people as numerous as Israel, but that night he has a dream that fulfills his deepest wish:

> The king went to Gibeon to sacrifice there, for it was the largest shrine. Solomon presented a thousand burnt offerings on that altar. At Gibeon the Lord appeared to Solomon

in a dream at night; and God said, "Ask, what shall I give you?" Solomon said, "You have been greatly loyal to your servant my father David, as he walked before you in loyalty and righteousness and integrity of heart. And you have sustained this great loyalty, giving him a son to sit on his throne as of this day. And now. Lord, my King, you have made your servant king in place of my father David, but I am a young man, a pip-squeak, who does not know how to come out or go in. Your servant is in the midst of the people you selected, a people too numerous to be numbered or counted. Give your servant an attentive mind to judge your people, to understand between good and evil, for who can judge this immense people of yours?" The request pleased the Lord. . . . Then Solomon awoke; it had been a dream. [1 Kings 3:4–15]

This is the only dream of Solomon's recorded in the biblical text, and given the importance of dreams as a record of the unconscious, the passage would seem ripe for the kind of analysis we are practicing here. Unfortunately for such an approach, while biblical authors anticipated Freud in believing that dreams sometimes encode their messages, Solomon's dream does not seem to hint at any hidden meaning. Dreams as understood in the ancient Near East were expressions not of the unconscious but of the divine will—kings would try to induce them for this reason, in fact, doing so by sleeping in the Temple (a practice known as dream incubation), and some scholars suspect that Solomon did something similar to induce this dream. Whatever merit that hypothesis has, the kind of dream that he has seems typically ancient Near Eastern in other respects, a dream in which the divine, not the psyche, reveals itself. Born of a different understanding of psychology than the one that Freud developed, the dream at Gibeon seems impervious to psychoanalytic interpretation—there are no uncanny symbols that Freudian dreams use to encrypt repressed desire—and with nothing in the dream to decode, we have no way into the preconscious impulses that generated it.

But this is to focus on the dream's surface, its manifest content in Freudian terms, and if we dig deeply enough, we might yet find something buried underneath. Freud argued that words in a dream often have a double meaning, as when he once dreamed of his son babbling nonsense words he did not understand only to recall later that they were garbled variants of long-forgotten Jewish words that he had absorbed from the Exodus story and that conveyed a secret message about Freud's Jewish identity. If we attend to what lies beneath the surface of dreamed-of words in this way, we find in Solomon's dream at least one example of a similar kind of unconscious linguistic play, a phrase that has more meaning than Solomon realized at the time: "Give your servant an attentive mind to judge your people, *to understand between good and evil.*"

What is potentially significant here is the phrase "to understand between good and evil" because it does in fact have a secondary meaning as a euphemism for sexual experience or ability. The same basic idiom underlies the Tree of Knowledge of Good and Evil in the Garden of Eden, and its sexual resonance seems relevant there as well, for when Adam and Eve eat of the fruit, the effect is closer to sexual self-consciousness than to moral awareness: their eyes are opened, they realize they are naked, and they cover themselves with fig leaves. I doubt Solomon consciously meant to allude to the Garden of Eden story, but if we follow the unconscious logic of dreams, tending to a word's hidden associations more than to its superficial denotation, the allusion points us to something deeper in the dream— what Freud might have called a "latent dream thought," and what Zornberg calls an "idiom of the unthinkable"—unconscious wishes not openly or directly expressed in language but that have left linguistic traces that we can track to their source.

I propose that Solomon's dream is a kind of palimpsest, another oft-used Freudian metaphor that describes a way in which a conscious memory or dream can conceal another, more ancient narrative underneath. The story that is hidden under

Solomon's dream is the Garden of Eden story, which, as many interpreters have recognized, is itself a palimpsest concealing beneath its words a memory of a child's formative experiences. Every character within the Eden story seems to correspond to some aspect of a developing child's mental processes, as if the story were an allegory for the maturation process. The serpent, of course, is the archetypal phallic symbol, introducing sexuality into human experience, while God plays the role of the Freudian superego, the overbearing conscience that sternly warns against giving into temptation and that punishes desire for acting on its impulses. For us, though, the character that is of most interest is Eve, for she, more than Adam, is the closest counterpart to Solomon himself by virtue of her desire for wisdom: "When the woman saw that the tree was good for eating and a delight to the eyes, *and that the tree was desireable to make one wise*, she took of its fruit." Eve is the true protagonist in the Garden of Eden story—she is the one that the serpent approaches, and she makes the key decision; Adam simply responds to her initiative—and what drives her is the same desire that surfaces in Solomon's dream, a wish for wisdom, which is why in our interpretation of the Eden story as the underside of that dream, it is she, not Adam, who functions as the king's alter ego.

What, then, can we learn by interpreting the Eden story as Solomon's dream?

We can see, first of all, that there is something adolescent about the king's desire for wisdom. Solomon describes himself in the dream as a young man who does not yet know how "to go out or come in"—perhaps a way of saying that he lacks military experience but also conceivably an admission of sexual inexperience. Early interpreters surmised, in fact, that he must have been in early adolescence at the time—he was fourteen, according to the early Jewish historian Josephus; twelve, according to the rabbis, and this too is what makes Eve a good stand-in for him, for she seems to be around the same age. Elsewhere in the Bible, in Deuteronomy 1:39 to be precise, mention is made of children who do not yet know good and evil, a reference to children under the age of twenty who have not yet had sexual experience. That would imply that Eve was in her teenage years at the time that she ate of the Tree of Knowledge, and her experience in doing so is that of an adolescent undergoing sexual awakening. She does not yet know good and evil at the beginning of the story but is easily tempted to partake of such knowledge, and when she does so she suddenly becomes aware of herself as a sexual being: "The eyes of both of them were opened, and they saw that they were naked" (Genesis 3:7).

To detect something sexual in the desire for wisdom might seem a great stretch at first, but a connection between the two kinds of desire has long been recognized. Curiosity, related to the word for care, originally meant diligence or attention to detail, but it was also often associated with sexual appetite. In fact, it was explicitly described as a kind of lust, the "lust of the eyes," as Augustine described it, or the *libido sciendi* as later scholars would refer to it, the lust to know. In a number of writings, Freud speaks of the *Wissbegierde*, an overpowering, greedy appetite for knowledge, which is really a German equivalent to libido sciendi, and he understood it to be an outgrowth of the libido, of the sex drive, tracing scientific inquisitiveness back to a child's sexual curiosity. Indeed, Freud recognized this impulse as the source of his own interest in medicine.

Reading the Garden of Eden story as a projection of Solomon's unconscious sexual urges suggests that his desire for wisdom isn't simply political; it is also pubescent, reflecting the emergence of sexual desire in a teenage king. The desire for wisdom isn't libidinous in any obvious sense, but it does share much in common with sexual desire—both represent a yearning to transcend the self, to penetrate the mystery of the other, to acquire forbidden knowledge—and for that reason the two desires can be hard to distinguish, as they are, for example, in the Song of Songs, the eroticized fantasies of a young Solomon according to one midrashic tradition. To many readers the song expresses a Gnostic reaching for divine wisdom, for ultimate understanding; Freud, on the other hand, read the song as an expression of sexual curiosity. The song is open to both readings because each kind of longing is so easily translated into the other. In the Garden of Eden story, the two desires converge in the phrase "knowing Good and Evil," and the repetition of the same idiom in Solomon's dream suggests they are fused there as well, that the king's desire for wisdom somehow relates to the emergence of sexuality.

If there is a sexual drive at the core of Solomon's desire for wisdom, however, why does it not express itself more directly? A skeptic might argue that it is so hard to detect because it isn't there at all, but a Freudian approach allows for another possibility; maybe Solomon has repressed it, his mind driving its shameful or disturbing impulses from itself as Adam and Eve are driven from the garden. Here again, in fact, we can look to the Eden story as an enactment of the psychological process at work. The moment that Eve and Adam partake of the Tree of Knowledge, they feel ashamed. They do not need to wait for God to punish them before they realize that they have done something wrong; they seem to intuitively understand that having given into temptation was a catastrophic mistake, and their impulsive response is to conceal—to cover themselves up with clothes and hide among the trees when they hear God approaching. If this is not the first act of repression in the history of humanity, it certainly illustrates it in an archetypal way.

We cannot prove that the young Solomon sought to repress his emergent sexual desires, but we do know from other sources that such desire was seen as extremely dangerous. In the book of Proverbs, for example, acting on one's sexual desire

can be fatal. The teacher quoted there, traditionally understood as Solomon, sternly warns his adolescent pupils against
succumbing to the temptation of the seductive adulteress who
sounds at first as if she comes from the Song of Songs—"Come
let us drink deeply of our love until morning," she calls out to
her lover (Proverbs 7:18)—but whose enticements are a trap:
the one who follows her is "like an ox going to slaughter"
(7:22). A wise man, Proverbs teaches, is wary of his sexual impulses; he restrains them and keeps his thoughts focused on
wisdom and never allows them to go astray. The wise aren't
asked to become monks—they can marry—but the women
judged acceptable by Proverbs are largely desexualized, figures
like the famous "woman of valor" who is praised at great length
in Proverbs 31 but who is of interest for her work ethic and wisdom, not her sex appeal.

If this is the kind of wisdom that Solomon acquired—and
after all, Proverbs is supposed to be a record of his thoughts—
we can understand what happened to the sexual impulse that
we detected in his dream. Solomon's desire for wisdom may
have been rooted in his libido, but the moment that he acquired
it is also the moment that he would have begun repressing it,
much as Adam and Eve feel ashamed of their nakedness at the
moment that they eat the forbidden fruit, because wisdom
teaches that sexual desire is dangerous, that it must be con-
trolled, curbed, replaced by the desire for wisdom. And this is
the Solomon that awakes from the dream—whatever emergent
sexual desire might have been taking shape in his unconscious
can nowhere be detected in his behavior as it is described in the
chapters that follow 1 Kings 3; from this point forward, he
seems the ultimate superego figure—the authoritative, impartial judge. He encounters several women over the course of his
story—the daughter of Pharaoh whom he marries in 1 Kings 3
before his dream, the two prostitutes who come before him in
the second half of that chapter, and the Queen of Sheba, who

visits him in 1 Kings 10—but he shows no sexual interest in any of them, as if he had completely expunged the libido that was so strong in his father and brothers.

But if Freud's understanding of the mind is correct, the sexual desire that we detected in Solomon's dream would not have completely disappeared; it was merely in hiding, waiting for a chance to come out into the open, and so it eventually does, at the end of Solomon's life, in behavior one would never expect from the author of Proverbs: "Solomon loved many foreign women—the daughter of Pharaoh: Moabite, Ammonite, Edomite, Sidonian, and Hittite women" (1 Kings 11:1). Suddenly, the king succumbs to the reckless, transgressive sexuality we found elsewhere in his family—in fact, Solomon's amorousness far surpasses that of his father and his brothers, seeming to know no limit.

How do we account for such a sudden and unexpected explosion of sexual desire?

If we have to stick to the surface of the text there is no way to explain why a figure as wise as Solomon would behave in this way. We can make sense of things, however, if we don't stick to that surface, if we posit for Solomon the kind of hidden mental life that we have reconstructed here. The desires of childhood can operate in a deferred fashion, argued Freud; they might recede into the unconscious during childhood itself, but they do not disappear, sometimes coming back in adulthood as compulsive, repetitive behavior. Solomon's behavior can be understood in this way. For much of his life, he scarcely seems to have any sexual desire, and then, as if out of nowhere, it explodes. We will see later that there are other ways to understand Solomon's polygamous perversity, but one possible explanation is a psychological one: the repetitiveness of Solomon's libido—his love of one woman after another in a nearly endless sequence—can be understood as a sign of repression which can intensify ordinary sexual desire, the prerational desire that we briefly glimpsed in the king's adolescent dream, now overpowering and insatiable.

This at least is how a Freudian might reconstruct the history of Solomon's psychological development, but I have to admit that while I am fascinated by Freudianism and its particular strain of intellectual ambition, I am by no means wholly convinced that it actually possesses the power that it claims for itself. Seeking to know the mind's deepest secrets is reaching for knowledge that is by definition unknowable (the "unconscious" is a translation of the German *Unbewusste*, the Unknown), and to acquire that kind of knowledge requires nothing less than Solomonic power, as Freud acknowledged in the *Psychopathology of Everyday Life*, in which he notes that the ability to interpret the cryptic behavior of people made one feel like Solomon, who according to legend was able to understand the cryptic language of animals. But humans cannot comprehend what animals say among themselves, and the analogy acknowledges something magical—that is, fantastical and implausible—about psychoanalysis and its power to interpret the hidden language of the mind's animal instincts—a claim to impossible knowledge that goes beyond what can really be known.

Whatever secrets it may disclose about Solomon's childhood or desire to be wise, psychoanalysis does reveal something else about the king—his role in later imaginations as a symbol of vaulting inquisitiveness, the lust to know. Whether there is any real affinity between Solomon's desire for wisdom, and the libido sciendi felt by Freud and other scientists, Freud's recognition of a similarity between himself and his Solomon speaks to one of the reasons we still tell the king's story. For the last four hundred years or so, for the entire history of modern science, Solomon has served as an important paradigm for scientific inquiry, his wisdom a symbol of the hidden or forbidden knowledge that scientists feel compelled to uncover. How is it that a religious figure like Solomon, a sage whose wisdom comes from God, could become a scientific hero? The answer leads into one of the most fascinating aspects of Solomon's biography as a cultural symbol, a history that involves Columbus, Newton, and other pivotal figures in the history of exploration and science.

But we will get to all that a bit later; there is another story that I must tell first. To understand why Solomon needed wisdom—not just why he lusted after it but why he *needed* it in a very practical sense—we have to understand how he became king. Here too there seems to be more going on than the Bible reports, but the subtext that we seek to uncover this time is not psychological but political, a secret plot that certain readers have detected between the lines of the official account of how King Solomon came to power.

3

---◆◄◆►◆---

Succession Struggles

BEFORE SOLOMON COULD BECOME an all-knowing sage, he
had to become king of Israel, and that was no easy position to
acquire. In Chronicles, his succession to power is seamless—
David designates Solomon his heir, and he ascends to the
throne without controversy or conflict. Kings presents a different story; there, the young prince is not the first or most likely
candidate to succeed David, and he must first win the support
of David himself and then overcome the opposition of some
dangerous foes before he can take the throne. Not even the
greatest leaders in Israelite history had ever successfully passed
power onto a son, not Moses or the prophet Samuel or Saul
(even though he had a first-rate successor in Jonathan), nor was
Solomon the most likely person to inherit the throne successfully given his status as a younger son of a disreputable mother.
The fact that he not only obtained power in such a society but
prevailed, outlasting better positioned rivals to emerge as one

of history's most accomplished kings, suggests that in addition to being smart, Solomon was also exceedingly savvy.

In this chapter I will tell the history of this succession—the power struggles that led up to it and the way in which Solomon consolidated his rule—but I do not want merely to paraphrase the narrative in 1 Kings 1–2, for there is reason to think that this account isn't the whole story. In the view of most scholars, what we have preserved in these chapters is a work of royal propaganda, the so-called Succession Narrative, thought to have been composed during the reign of Solomon himself. It was supposedly compiled by an eyewitness to the events that it describes, perhaps a royal scribe, but its author was hardly a nonpartisan observer, describing the succession in a way designed to overcome misgivings about how the king came to power. If this reconstruction is correct, then we can recount only the "official" story of how Solomon came to power, the story as it was told by the king's own spin doctors.

If one compares the Succession Narrative with other similar ancient Near Eastern narratives, however, something surprising emerges. Other ancient peoples also told stories of how their kings came to power, and their portraits are invariably flattering, depicting the king in question as an extraordinary individual selected by the gods to rule on their behalf. That is very close to what we have in 1 Kings, but what is unusual about its account is the way it raises questions about Solomon's legitimacy, never outwardly challenging the image of him as a divinely elected leader but nevertheless planting seeds of doubt.

It is hard to know whether these subversive elements in the story are deliberate. The East German writer Stefan Heym, in a novel titled the *King David Report*, suggested that they were, imagining the narrative's author as a morally conflicted scribe named Ethan the Ezrahite (inspired by the mention of such a scribe in 1 Kings 5:11) commissioned by Solomon to produce an official account of the king's history but feeling compelled to smuggle in the truth of what really happened—the cowardice, the sexual perversion, the suppression of opponents, and the manipulation of the historical record. Heym's understanding of 1 Kings reflects his own experience living under Communist rule, and the idea of the biblical author as a literary saboteur seems anachronistic in the context of the ancient Near East, where most scribes worked at the bidding of the powers that be. Heym's interpretation was not without basis in the biblical text, however, for there are ways in which 1 Kings itself hints at some kind of conspiracy behind Solomon's rise to power, a hidden plot that involved the prophet Nathan, Bathsheba, and perhaps—though it is impossible to pin anything specific on him—young Prince Solomon himself.

Heirs Apparent and Inapparent

We begin the story not with Solomon himself but with another pretender to the throne: Adonijah, Solomon's brother, who is convinced that he is the one destined to become Israel's king. In fact, even before David's death he begins to act like a king by riding around Jerusalem in a parade preceded by horses, chariots, and fifty bodyguards. We cannot tell whether Adonijah was the oldest surviving son of David at this point, but he is almost certainly older than Solomon, and he has another quality that recommends him as a prospective king as well—good looks—a trait that distinguished the previous two kings, Saul and David, but not, so far as we can tell, Solomon.

Adonijah also has the support of powerful allies. Two of Israel's most powerful leaders back him: the priest Abiathar and the general Joab. To have the blessing of Abiathar was to be aligned not only with David himself, who has had a close relationship with Abiathar since his days as a fugitive from Saul, but with ancient Israelite religious tradition, for Abiathar is the heir to an ancient and prestigious priestly line, the house of Eli, which tended to the ark of the covenant before David brought it to Jerusalem. Joab is David's most effective military commander, the one who actually did the dirty work for him by eliminating enemies like Uriah and Absalom though he was always careful to draw suspicion away from David. Joab is so dangerous that David himself felt powerless to act against him—and now he is on Adonijah's side.

Adonijah's strategy for becoming king was based on a recognition of politics as a performatory art, a kind of theater. He needed strong allies to be sure, but Adonijah's main strategy is to become king by appearing to be a king—declaring himself king, running around with a royal bodyguard, performing the kind of rituals that kings perform (one suspects the influence of Joab here; he always had his eye on how David was perceived publicly). The next step in this strategy was a public sacrifice conducted at a stone near the site of En-rogel, a spring just outside of Jerusalem. The sacrifice was staged as an elaborate public feast to which Adonijah invited his brothers and other important members of the king's court, probably seeking to win them over in this way and perhaps even hoping to be publicly acclaimed as king before the end of the festivities.

Adonijah made just one mistake; he neglected to invite Solomon and his supporters. He might have done so on purpose, suspecting that they opposed him as king, but their exclusion proved an opportunity for them, for, left behind in Jerusalem, they could act out of sight, without giving Adonijah a chance to preempt their plan.

At the head of Solomon's faction is the prophet Nathan, who had taken a special interest in the prince since the latter's birth. David had remained silent when Adonijah first began acting like king, and his quiescence must have encouraged the prince in his royal pretensions, but David had not actually declared him to be his successor, and that meant that his endorsement was still up for grabs. Adonijah's absence from Jerusalem meant that Nathan could focus on securing this support for Solomon. In a patrilineal society like ancient Israel, where a man's status as heir was conferred on him by the blessing of his father, there could be no stronger source of legitimacy for Solomon than to be recognized by David as his rightful heir, and that is what Nathan now set out to arrange.

Nathan does not initially approach David himself, however. The last time he spoke to the king was to announce the death of his child as punishment for his affair with Bathsheba, and one could reasonably assume that the king would not be happy to see him again. Rather than go directly to David, therefore, Nathan turns to a surrogate, Bathsheba, using her relationship to the king to lay the groundwork for his own petition:

> Nathan said to Bath-sheba, Solomon's mother: "Have you not heard that Adonijah son of Haggith has become king and our lord David does not know it. Now come, let me advise you so that you can save your own life and the life of your son Solomon. Go, approach David and say to him, 'Did you not, my lord king, swear to your servant, saying: "Your son Solomon shall rule and become king after me, and he will sit on my throne? Why then has Adonijah become king?"' While you are talking there to the king, I will come in after you and confirm your words." [1 Kings 1:11–14]

While we cannot know for certain, Nathan could be advising Bathsheba to lie. The questionable part of his instructions is his request that she remind the king of a vow to make Solomon king. It is certainly possible that David really made such a promise, but the vow is nowhere mentioned in the preceding narrative, and we know that Nathan has misled David before, tricking him into denouncing himself after his affair with Bathsheba. It is thus conceivable that he misleads him here too, inventing the oath in the hope that a doddering king would not recall well enough to deny making it.

Bathsheba does as she is told, but she proves to be a cunning figure in her own right. She hasn't said anything in the narrative thus far—unless one accepts the tradition that it was she who gave her son the name Solomon—but now she must act to save herself and her son, and she does so in a way that reveals unsuspected initiative:

> My lord, you swore by the Lord your God to your servant, saying, "Your son Solomon shall succeed me as king, and he shall sit on my throne." But now look, Adonijah has become king, and now you, my lord king, did not know it. He has sacrificed oxen, fatted cattle and sheep in abundance, and has invited all the sons of the king, the priest Abiathar, and Joab the commander of the army, but your servant Solomon he has not invited. But you, my lord the king, the eyes of all Israel are on you to tell them who will sit on the throne of my lord the king after him. Otherwise, when my lord lays down with his fathers [that is, when he dies], my son Solomon and I myself will be thought sinners. [1 Kings 1:17–21]

Bathsheba's initiative is reflected in how she supplements and improves on Nathan's instructions. Following his instructions, she mentions the vow, but she adds a detail that the prophet never mentioned, describing it as an oath taken in the name of the Lord. If David really made such a promise, it is possible that she makes the addition because she remembers better than Nathan did what he actually said to her, but if the oath is a fabrication, her addition represents a small but significant improvement that makes it that much more difficult for David to go back on what he is being told he promised.

Other additions introduced by Bathsheba suggest a shrewd attempt to play on the king's insecurities. Consider the statement "But now look, Adonijah has become king, and now you, my lord king, *did not know it.*" David had always prided himself on being in the know, so the idea that Adonijah was doing something without his knowledge no doubt irritated him, but even more humiliating was the sexual implication of this statement. Earlier in the scene, before Bathsheba's appearance, we learn that David may have been afflicted by his declining mastery of another kind of "knowledge"—knowledge as a euphemism for sexual ability.

> King David was getting on in years. They covered him with clothes, but he couldn't stay warm, so his servants said to him, "Let a young virgin be sought for my lord; she can stand before the king and be his attendant. She can lie in your bosom and my lord the king will stay warm." They sought a beautiful girl throughout all the territory of Israel, and they found Abishag the Shunammite, and they brought her to the king. The girl was extremely beautiful. She became the king's attendant and served him, *but the king did not know her.* [1 Kings 1:1–4]

The Bible doesn't actually report that David was impotent, but according to the Talmud at least, that was how Abishag herself—the beautiful companion of David's old age—understood his refusal to have sex with her. In a story told in the Babylonian Talmud, in tractate *Sanhedrin* 22a, Abishag pushes for David to marry her, but he refuses on the grounds that he already has eighteen wives—the maximum number of wives allowed a king according to Jewish tradition. Abishag doesn't believe him, however, accusing him of making excuses for his impotence, and the charge so humiliates David that he feels he has to prove his manhood by summoning Bathsheba to his room to have sex with her thirteen times and then proving this to Abishag by showing her the handkerchief that bears the traces of his sexual emissions. The Bathsheba of 1 Kings knows better than to shame David in such a direct way (especially in the presence of Abishag, who, according to 1 Kings 1:15, is in the room too), but she was in an excellent position to know

David's sexual secrets, and her use of the verb "know" might well represent a covert challenge to his virility: Adonijah shows his virility, while you, David, you prove yourself impotent.

We cannot of course be certain that any of these subtle maneuvers are really there in the text, that we were intended to detect them. On the surface, Nathan and Bathsheba are simply petitioning the king to honor a promise he has really made, and there is nothing in what they say that need be read as underhanded or double-edged. But reading their words in this way is consistent with their overall approach to the problem of succession. Whereas Adonijah's tactics are overt and performatory, relying on open declarations and exhibitions, Nathan and Bathsheba work surreptitiously, behind the scenes (much as the author of the narrative does, perhaps not coincidentally) and the ploys that we have discerned between the lines of their petition would be consistent with this, concealing their true intentions even from David himself.

And in contrast to Adonijah's theatrical methods, this more covert strategem works. Roused from his torpor by the words of Bathsheba and Nathan—or shamed into taking action by Bathsheba's sexual insinuations—the king responds in exactly the way that they were hoping for, affirming his promise to make Solomon king: "As the Lord lives, who has saved my life from every adversity, as I swore to you by the Lord, the God of Israel, 'Your son Solomon shall become king after me, and he shall sit on my throne in my place,' so will I do this day" (1 Kings 1:30–31). At this point, Solomon's camp can go public with their claim, which is exactly what they do, quickly staging an anointing ritual by which the young Solomon is acclaimed king, but there is something secretive even about the new king's coronation, which is done in a rushed way and without the knowledge of Adonijah and his supporters. They are just completing their sacrificial feast as Solomon is being anointed king, and when they hear the noise of his coronation coming from Jerusalem, they have no idea what is going on.

Joab, the likely mastermind behind Adonijah's campaign to become king, is the first to recognize that something was wrong—"Why is the city in such an uproar?"—and no sooner does he pose the question then a messenger appears to announce the news: "Alas, our lord David has made Solomon king." That is all it takes for the performance Adonijah has worked so hard to orchestrate to fall apart: everyone flees for their lives, including Adonijah himself, who instantly abandons his pose of bravado as he dashes in a panic to the altar of the Lord in the hope of gaining asylum there. Solomon and his supporters never have to risk a direct confrontation with Adonijah—they do not have to fight him or even threaten him—because Adonijah's power is entirely illusory, a stage performance, and all that is necessary to overcome it is to disrupt the script it was supposed to follow.

Solomon, the narrative wants us to believe, is a very different kind of figure. His power does not depend on appearance—on his good looks or on any attempt to simulate the attributes of a king. In contrast to Adonijah, he never engages in any public relations campaign, never cultivates an impression of himself as a warrior or a judge; we never so much as hear him give a speech—he leaves it to others to make his case for him. He comes to power, in other words, not through the manipulation of appearances but through the ability to operate behind appearances, which makes one notice, come to think of it, that Solomon himself has remained out of sight during this whole episode, except for the end, when he is anointed king. Without giving it much thought, most readers would attribute his absence to his youth—he is simply too young to play an active role in politics, requiring his mother and other patrons to look out for his best interest—but this is Solomon we are speaking about, already recognized as exceptionally wise even as a young man, and that wisdom allows for another possibility. Might Solomon be missing from the story of his succession not because he is too young or too passive but because he understands even better than Nathan and Bathsheba how to hide a plot, concealing his own political maneuvers in a place where even the biblical author cannot detect them?

A Crooked Path to Wisdom

Apart from teaching us how Solomon came to power, the behind-the-scenes perspective that 1 Kings affords us suggests that the new king's emerging interest in wisdom was not only personal but also tactical. The House of David, like many other royal families, was a realm of hidden plots and false appearances, and a key survival skill in this kind of environment was the ability to detect the secrets of others. David was a master of this skill. He too was known for his wisdom as we have noted—"knowing everything on the earth"—but what that means in context is a knowledge of everything happening within his realm, including the scheming of his enemies. The same kind of knowledge is what gives Solomon the edge against Adonijah. His side knows what Adonijah is doing, as if there was some spy concealed among his supporters, while Adonijah does not have a clue about what Solomon's camp is up to until it is too late.

But Solomon's wisdom in this context is not yet the divine insight that God grants him in 1 Kings 3. The Solomon of 1 Kings 1–2 is described as wise—when a dying David refers to Solomon as a "wise man" in 1 Kings 2:9, he is using the same word for wisdom, *hakham*, that will be used for Solomon's wisdom after 1 Kings 3—but Solomon's wisdom in this context seems to reflect some other form of understanding that is far more political and practical, far more human, than the wisdom that helped the king resolve impossible court cases and perform other feats of supernatural sagacity. It is this pre-wisdom wisdom of Solomon that we will try to pin down in the rest of this chapter. What is it that the young king understood, and how does this understanding relate to the divine wisdom bestowed on him in 1 Kings 3, the wisdom for which he is now famous?

Before we try to answer these questions, however, let us first pick up the thread of the narrative in 1 Kings 2. Solomon's first act as king occurs just after Adonijah seeks asylum at the altar of the Lord. The prince has grabbed hold of the altar's horns and refuses to let go until *King* Solomon (so Adonijah refers to him now) swears not to put him to the sword. Solomon's response, the first words from him ever cited in the Bible, suggests the fairness and temperance that we might expect of the king. "If he is a worthy man, not one of his hairs will fall to the ground, but if wickedness is found in him, he shall die" (1 Kings 1:52). Adonijah's first words in the narrative were an expression of unabashed self-interest: "I will be king," with an emphasis on the "I." In contrast, Solomon's first words employ a neutral third person, and he speaks with the impersonal authority of the law—in fact, his sentence structure is characteristic of the kinds of laws found in the book of Exodus. There is not a trace here of anger or personal resentment, just a somewhat detached sense that justice must be done, tempered by a willingness to give Adonijah a second chance.

Solomon shows similar restraint in dealing with other enemies. Even before he threw his support behind Adonijah, Joab had given Solomon plenty of reasons to feel threatened by him; and yet Solomon does not act against Joab either, or the priest Abiathar, or any other supporter of Adonijah. David had been worried about yet another potential threat, Shimei of the House of Saul, one of the last surviving members of that earlier dynasty. In 2 Samuel 16, as David was fleeing Absalom during the latter's revolt, Shimei seized on his vulnerability to

publicly renounce the king, declaring his misfortunes a punishment for his crimes against the family of Saul. Shimei's very
existence reminded the people that David was a usurper, and
that there were alternatives to whom they might turn, which is
why, in his last words to Solomon, David urges his son to send
Shimei to his grave—not just as payback for a public insult but
as a preemptive effort to snuff out any potential revival of Saul's
dynasty after his death. But what does Solomon actually do
once he had the power to act on his father's last wishes? He
does order Shimei not to leave Jerusalem on the penalty of
death, but otherwise he leaves him alone as well, so that even
Shimei himself acknowledges that he is being treated well.

In his first acts as king, in other words, Solomon seems already to embody the kind of wisdom with which he is associated—an impartial, impersonal commitment to justice. If he
had been younger and stronger, David would have used the opportunity to punish or eliminate his enemies. Not so Solomon:
he refrains from violence, putting the need for justice over his
own need for vengeance or self-defense. But this is to take the
narrative at face value, and again, there is reason to suspect
something more sinister going on behind the scenes. Whatever doubts we might have about Nathan or Bathsheba, Solomon himself hasn't done anything to make us distrustful of
him, but one suspicious coincidence has led readers to wonder
if he is as committed to justice as he seems: despite Solomon's
forbearance, all of his enemies end up dead anyway.

The first to go is Adonijah. Sometime after he is spared by
Solomon, Adonijah falls in love with Abishag, David's concubine, and seeks permission to marry her. Wanting to sleep with
the king's concubine was a dangerously subversive act. During
his rebellion against his father, Absalom, following the advice
of the sage Ahitophel, made a deliberate decision to sleep with
his father's concubines as a way of shaming his father and claiming his throne. Adonijah's desire to marry Abishag could easily

be seen as a similar act of defiance, but that does not seem to have been his intention: he is so desperate for her, in fact, that he risks seeking the help of Bathsheba, the mother of his rival, asking her to petition her son on his behalf, and he assures her that he has no desire to become king. Unfortunately for him, Bathsheba fails to mention this disavowal during her petition, and in Solomon's mind it makes Adonijah's attempt to marry Abishag an act of treason. He had promised to spare him on the condition that he commit no wickedness, and Adonijah had accepted the condition, making their relationship a kind of covenant, and just as God is justified in punishing Israel when it violates its covenant, so too is Solomon when he sentences Adonijah to death for breaking his promise.

Next to go are Adonijah's most powerful supporters, Abiathar and Joab. Probably because Abiathar was a close associate of David's, sharing in many of his hardships, Solomon was content to spare him despite his support of a political rival, but once he is able to move against Adonijah, Solomon realizes that it is time to move against Abiathar as well, removing him from his role as priest and exiling him to his family's estate outside Jerusalem. Lest we think that his actions are political payback, however, Solomon explains that he is simply acting to fulfill a divine promise. Abiathar was the descendant of an ancient priestly family, the priests of the temple of Shiloh, who had betrayed their sacred trust by acting in corrupt ways, and their actions so angered God that he promised to wipe out the family except for one descendant who would be spared only so that he could bear witness to the tragic demise of his lineage. As it turns out, most of the priests of Shiloh were violently exterminated by King Saul, who sought to punish them for helping David escape his clutches, but Abiathar alone managed to escape, serving as the chief priest of Jerusalem until he made the mistake of supporting Adonijah. His exile, Solomon explains, was not to punish him for that support, but merely to fulfill the ancient curse on his family, a divine punishment imposed long before Solomon's birth.

With Joab, he exhibits no mercy whatsoever. Once he realized that he was in trouble, the general too rushed to the altar of the Lord, not just to seek God's mercy but because according to a widely respected custom, he should have been immune to violence as long as he was in contact with the altar. Throughout the ancient world, criminals fled to temples to seek asylum, knowing that they were under the protection of the gods while they remained in contact with an object or place that belonged to them. Even powerful kings were reluctant to anger the gods by violating the sanctity of their holy places. The commander Benaiah hesitates to kill Joab for this reason, but Solomon is indifferent to such concerns and orders him to strike down Joab at the altar itself, and what justifies such a brazen act is the blood on Joab's head. He had killed two men who were more righteous than himself, Abner, son of Ner, and Amasa, son of Jether, and striking Joab down was the only way for Solomon to ensure that the bloodshed would end, that Solomon's own kin would not be held responsible for Joab's crimes, that justice is done.

This leaves one last enemy, Shimei of the House of Saul, who has kept silent since Solomon confined him to Jerusalem. Three years after Solomon spared him on the condition that he never leave Jerusalem, however, Shimei makes a fateful choice: two of his slaves have run away to the city of Gath, and he decides to track them down, apparently either forgetting that leaving Jerusalem would bring a death sentence or thinking that the punishment would not apply in this instance since he intended to return. But Solomon hasn't forgotten what Shimei did to his father, nor is it likely that he missed the political implications of Shimei's journey (Saul himself had once gone on a similar journey, going out in search of runaway donkeys, and it was during that trek that he was anointed king). When Solomon orders Shimei's execution, however, his justification is not political but pious; it is bad enough that Shimei broke his promise to Solomon, but that promise (the king only now discloses) was an oath taken in the name of the Lord, which turns its violation into a grave religious offense and thus makes Shimei all the more deserving of the fate he is about to suffer.

In each of these episodes, Solomon appears completely justified in his actions; either he had warned his victims beforehand, imposing reasonable conditions that they then violated, or else he had ample moral or religious justification for his actions—the blood that Joab shed, an ancient curse on the family of Abiathar that doomed his line to extinction. Difficult to ignore, however, is how much Solomon stood to gain from these deaths. With Adonijah still alive, his own claim to the throne would never be secure. With Abiathar still in a position of priestly influence, he could never completely count on the support of the priesthood for his own rule or, conceivably, for a temple he was planning. Joab was simply too dangerous to have around. And so long as Shimei was alive, people would be reminded that there had once been another royal family, the House of Saul, and might be tempted to restore it. The justifications that Solomon cites for getting rid of all these enemies seem like legal pretexts, attempts to excuse murders that would otherwise call into question the new king's claim to be just and peaceful.

We cannot demonstrate any criminality in a court of law, of course, but earlier interpreters believed that they could. Rabbinic tradition shows a surprising sympathy for those killed by Solomon in this period—Shimei becomes one of Solomon's teachers while Joab was remembered as a noble and generous figure whose death at the hands of Solomon was a heartbreaking tragedy. "Woe to the world if this be justice!" laments the Joab of this tradition when he learns that he is to die. Is there anything to the general's claim of injustice? According to rabbinic tradition, there are holes in Solomon's case against him. The king lacked the two witnesses required by the Torah for a conviction in a capital trial, and while Joab certainly sent a number of people to their death, he may have had legal justification for doing so. Indeed, as if to make up for Solomon's disregard of proper legal procedure, the Talmud provides Joab with a trial in which, after hearing the general's defense of his actions, the judges reverse Solomon's judgment, acquitting him of one of the murders of which he was accused on the grounds that he committed it in self-defense (*Sanhedrin* 49a).

As discerning as he was, however, Solomon himself seems to have known how fishy all these deaths seemed, which explains why he works so hard to justify everything that he does. David too was able to justify the killings that made his rise possible, but he did not completely overcome the doubts of some. Shimei openly accused him of the death of Saul and his sons, for example, and such suspicions dogged David to his death. Solomon did not disguise what he did; he gave the orders himself, and yet no one accused him of any crime, perhaps because people were afraid to but also, it seems, because Solomon was so careful to make every death appear just, sparing his enemies at first and always with reasonable conditions that made their subsequent deaths seem deserved. The great chronicler of princely ambition, Niccolò Machiavelli, observed that it was unnecessary that a ruler be virtuous, but essential that he appear to be so. That Solomon could have acted in such a self-serving and brutal way, and yet is famous to this day for being just and peaceful, suggests he was a master of the art of appearing virtuous.

We are in a better position now to understand the pre-wisdom wisdom of the young Solomon. It is not yet the wisdom for which he is remembered in later religious tradition. It is not divinely inspired or supernatural, nor does it encompass mystical or magical insights beyond the reach of ordinary humans. Rather, it is a strain of worldly wisdom: Machiavellian cunning, street wisdom, a shrewd understanding of how to survive in a dangerous environment, of how to strike an enemy and get away with it.

How, then, did this unscrupulous and manipulative potentate become the exemplary sage now revered by three major religions? It is not the result of any kind of educational or maturational process; it happens suddenly, miraculously, as the result of divine intervention. Solomon goes to sleep one night, has the dream recorded in 1 Kings 3, and awakes a different man, no longer concerned with power struggles and newly endowed with intellectual powers that go well beyond the knowledge of anyone else. It is not certain that we can understand what happened to Solomon that night since, as mere mortals, we lack the insight to understand what it means to possess divine wisdom.

The rest of this book is devoted to understanding the Solomon that emerges from this dream, and he is indeed a very different figure than the one we have encountered in 1 Kings 1–2. Before we begin to tell his story, however, I would note that his newfound wisdom isn't completely disconnected from the wisdom that Solomon possess before the dream. We have seen, after all, that even before 1 Kings 3, Solomon professes to be an agent of impersonal justice, though justice at this point is not resolving conflict but making sure that one's enemies get what they deserve. It is said of Solomon after he receives divine wisdom that nothing is hidden from him, but he shows a knack for ferreting out hidden information earlier as well, always knowing what his enemies are up to. The Solomon who emerges after 1 Kings 3 knows no limits—his wisdom allows him to do whatever he desires to do—and this trait too is anticipated in 1 Kings 1–2. Most rulers would have refrained from dragging a supplicant from the altar of a god, but not Solomon, who is willing from the beginning to pursue objectives that should be left beyond reach.

In other words, while divine wisdom transforms the king in dramatic ways, it is also rooted in who he has always been, never completely transcending its prehistory as the cunning of a Machiavellian prince. As we turn now to consider that wisdom and all that it produced—the exceptional legal judgment, the books of Solomonic insight, the magical powers, the peace and prosperity, the Temple of Jerusalem—we can, if we look closely enough, recognize that the pre-wisdom wisdom of the young king Solomon never really disappears; it is hidden somewhere in all these accomplishments, transmuted into intellectual and spiritual endeavor, but still ambitious, audacious, and very dangerous.

4

————◆|◆|◆————

Solomonic Judgments

UNTIL MODERN TIMES, Solomon was so closely associated with wisdom that he was often referred to simply as "the wise man." Readers automatically knew who was being referred to without an author mentioning him by name. But what does it mean to be the supreme wise man in an age that places no special value on wisdom? As Gabriel Marcel and other philosophers have observed, wisdom itself has lost much of its allure and authority in modern times, eclipsed by scientific knowledge and professional expertise even in philosophy departments. Marcel saw this as an unfortunate development. I am not so sure myself. The ancient notion of wisdom was elitist and inaccessible. It originated among the gods, who could see things that humans could not because they were unconstrained by the limits of mortality. They shared it with humans but only with the select few—scholars and magicians who didn't concern themselves with everyday matters. Predictably, this concept of wisdom no longer garners much respect in a world that is secularized, democratic, and distrustful of intellectuals.

Even today, however, wisdom preserves a bit of her authority. Sage figures like Einstein and Freud inspire a certain reverence, and not simply because of what they have taught us but also because of the esoteric nature of their knowledge, their ability to penetrate aspects of nature or human experience that aren't visible to the rest of us. It may not be a coincidence, as the cultural historian Stephen Whitfield has observed, that many of our own culture's wisdom figures—benign, brilliant sages that we turn to for guidance through the labyrinths of life—happen to be noticeably Jewish, such as political advisers like Henry Kissinger, economic gurus like Alan Greenspan (before the recent economic downturn that tarnished his reputation for omniscience), and public advice-givers like Dr. Ruth Westheimer. The pronouncements of these figures, often given an authoritative, old-world cast by being expressed in the European accent of one's grandparents, are the modern equivalent to what the ancients defined as wisdom, as they discern patterns in the world, or in human behavior, that most of us do not recognize, and draw from that insight practical lessons for how to lead a better life.

Whitfield traces the ancestry of this figure back to the early modern period, to a stereotype of the Jew as possessing superior knowledge, and more specifically to literary characters like the title character in Gotthold Lessing's play *Nathan the Wise* or the Jewish scientist Joabin in Francis Bacon's utopia the *New Atlantis*. The latter figure is perhaps based on Joachim Gaunse, a metallurgist and mining engineer brought to Virginia by Sir Walter Raleigh in 1585 to help uncover the riches thought to lie buried there; Gaunse was not only the earliest Jewish expert in North America and the founder of its first science center, but also the first known Jew to set foot there. But the lineage of this figure goes back well beyond the beginnings of modernity to Solomon himself, who combines many of the essential features of modern wisdom figures: the all-knowing intellectual authority figure, with expertise in politics, money, medicine, and/or affairs of the heart, and with a knack for conveying this expertise in the form of pithy advice.

Even the smartest of these modern wisdom figures could not compare in wisdom with Solomon, however. The Bible compares him to the wisest Israelites of the day—Ethan the Ezrahite, and the sons of Mahol, Heman, Chalkol, and Darsa—and none can match the wisdom of Solomon, nor do any of the sages of Egypt, despite their famed wisdom, or the Kedemites, the erudite scholars of Babylon and other ancient Mesopo-tamian centers of learning. And that was when the acquisition of wisdom was the goal of every intellectual. In an age that has largely lost interest in wisdom, today's sages could not hope to compare, as God seems to anticipate when he declares the king wiser than anyone who had come before or who would ever be.

So what was it that Solomon knew that the rest of us do not? It is commonly assumed today that wisdom comes from experience—note that many of the modern wisdom figures mentioned above are elderly, speaking with the authority of age and perspective—but experience isn't the source of Solomon's wisdom. He acquired his wisdom while still a young man and all at once, after a single night. His wisdom likewise does not reflect disciplined study, late-night reading, rigorous training, or the influence of a wise mentor—other ways in which a would-be sage might gain a measure of understanding. Solomon's wisdom is unique, unparalleled, and uncanny. This is why the narrative does not explain it or describe its contents in any detail—to do so would be to minimize its mystery—but only shows it in action, leaving us awestruck and puzzled just as it did the world of Solomon's day. But even so, perhaps by scrutinizing what little information is disclosed in 1 Kings, we might yet reach some understanding of what made Solomon's wisdom different from the garden variety sagacity of today's wisdom figures.

The most famous demonstration of Solomon's wisdom is, of course, the story of the two prostitutes in 1 Kings 3. It is there, as we have noted, that the young king is confronted with a truly impossible problem that would confound any other judge. Each of the two mothers had recently had a child, but the child of one died in the night, smothered by his mother as she slept. One of the mothers now accuses the other of switching the dead child for her living one: "The living son is mine, and the dead son is yours," but the other is just as insistent: "No, the dead son is yours, and the living one is mine." There are no witnesses, and so far as we can tell, there is nothing about either woman that makes one more credible than the other.

The only clue that Solomon might hope to discover lies in the testimony of the two women themselves. Perhaps the speech of one or the other of the women reveals some implausible detail, an inconsistency, a tic in the manner of presentation that might reveal the truth. But here too the evidence is inconclusive:

> The first woman said: "Please, my lord, I and this woman live in the same house, and I gave birth with her in the house. On the third day after I gave birth, this woman also gave birth. We were together; there was no one else with us in the house, only the two of us were in the house. But this woman's son died in the night because she lay on him. She got up in the middle of the night and took my son from beside me while your servant was sleeping. She laid him at her breast, and laid her dead son at my breast. I got up in the morning to nurse my son—and he was dead; but then when I looked at him closely in the morning, it was not the son I had born." But the other woman said, "No, my son is the living one and yours is the dead one." [1 Kings 3:17–22]

Many commentators find the first woman's account more credible because it is lengthier and more detailed, while the second woman's response is as spare as could be, as if she were afraid of saying something that might catch her up in a lie. But a shrewd detective could find much that is suspicious in the first woman's account. After all, if she was asleep when her child was taken, how does she know how the other woman's child died ("this woman's son died in the night *because she lay on him*")? Why did she not wake up when the other woman placed a dead child at her breast? And why does she have to look so closely at the dead child before recognizing that it is not her own?

In the face of a seemingly impossible puzzle, King Solomon cracks the case with a gesture that seems at first more brash than brilliant. His judgment has captivated imaginations ever since. In fact, the earliest known illustration of any biblical story is a depiction of this very episode. It was found in Italy, in the city of Pompey, on the wall of a house buried in the volcanic ash that destroyed the city in 79 C.E.

Solomon is on the right, sitting on the dais along with two other figures—probably fellow judges—and he is looking down on one of the two women as she kneels in supplication. The child is stretched out on a butcher's block, and a soldier dressed in what looks like a Roman uniform stands over him, poised to cut him in two. The second woman is at the child's side, already grabbing at her half. Various spectators look on, including two figures in the far left corner, two men rendered with great clarity, in whose faces it is possible to detect keen attention and perhaps admiration. Art historian Theodore Feder, noticing that the figure to the right rests his chin on his hand in the pose of a philosopher, has proposed that these are no ordinary onlookers but Socrates and Aristotle looking on with admiration at Solomon's judgment. The idea that Greek sages were present in Solomon's court may seem wildly anachronistic—the real Socrates and Aristotle lived centuries after the king—but

The earliest known illustration of Solomon's Judgment (or any biblical scene, for that matter), from the city of Pompey sometime before its destruction in 79 C.E. (Reprinted with permission from Art Resource)

it reflects a widespread view in late antiquity that Greek philosophy drew some of its deepest insights from the biblical wisdom of Solomon. Here, the presence of Greece's best-known sages, who appear to be thinking very carefully about what they are seeing, may be a way of signaling how exceptional Solomon's wisdom was: it left even the greatest philosophers impressed.

The fact that this scene shows up in a Roman city at such an early period, as if it were just another scene from pagan mythology, demonstrates just how famous the story of Solomon's judgment already was. By the first century C.E. it was known well beyond the borders of Judea, and ever since it has maintained its grip on the artistic imagination, inspiring innumerable illustrations ranging from a decoration of medieval manuscripts and Gothic cathedrals to paintings by Renaissance masters like Raphael, to contemporary renderings by artists like He Qi and Leslie Xuereb. The story remains so firmly planted within our collective memory even today that one can tell a joke based on the episode and assume listeners will get the punch line whether or not they have ever actually read the biblical text themselves, as in the following example:

> Two women came before the king seeking justice. The first pointed to a young man that they had dragged with them, and said, "Please, my lord, this man promised to marry my daughter and then reneged in order to marry this other woman's daughter." The other woman objected, "No, he promised to marry my daughter." They argued for some time, until finally the king said, "Fetch me a sword. I will cut the young man in two and give half to one and half to the other." The first woman cried out, "spare his life"; the second said, "Go ahead and cut." The king pointed to the second woman and said, "Behold, the true mother-in-law."

As well known as the biblical story is, however, and as hard as it may be to take it seriously now—we need to pretend that we have never encountered it before, paying very close attention to what the biblical text does and does not say to fully appreciate what it reveals about Solomon's wisdom. To begin with, notice that the king does not respond to the case in the way a judge would today. He does not ask any questions of the women or seek any evidence or testimony to confirm their stories; instead, he issues a simple order: "So the king said, 'Fetch me a sword,' and they brought a sword before the king. The king said, 'Cut the living boy in two, and give half to the one and half to the other'" (1 Kings 3:24–25). Imagine what it must have been like to hear this order given without yet knowing the story's famous resolution. Solomon is not yet famous for his wisdom; he is unknown and untested, and there is no reason to suspect that he does not mean what he says. According to the first century C.E. Jewish historian Josephus, those present to witness the case laughed to themselves when they saw Solomon's response, snickering at the young king's simpleminded effort to find a compromise. But perhaps the laughter Josephus thinks he hears is nervous laughter. One of the few things known about Solomon by this point is that he is quick to dispense justice with a sword. Why would such a ruler call for a sword now if he did not intend to use it? Reading the story with fresh eyes, we feel not admiration but the scorn and horror of Solomon's spectators, aghast that the new king could be so foolish and so cruel.

In a flash, however, our fears give way to wonder and relief. The two women speak up, and the truth is revealed. The first woman cries out in desperation, exhibiting the self-sacrificial instincts of maternal love: "Please, my lord, give her the living boy; do not kill him!" The second woman is impervious to the pain of the child and to the cry of her rival. She would sooner see the child die than cede him to the other woman, and so intent is she on punishing the other mother that even the prospect of having the child for herself does not move her: "It shall be neither mine nor yours; divide it." It is not hard to determine who the better mother is here; she is the more empathetic and caring individual. Identifying the actual mother, the biological mother, is another matter, however—genetic testing and polygraphs did not exist in biblical times—and this is the wondrous feat that Solomon's judgment accomplishes. His judgment does not merely produce the best outcome for the child; it uncovers a truth that should have been impossible to ascertain.

For centuries, biblical commentators have sought to explain how Solomon solved the case, scouring the story for clues. Rabbi Joseph Karo, a twelfth century scholar, suggested that Solomon would have been able to confirm whether the baby was as old as the first woman claimed (she claimed to give birth three days ahead of the other woman) by examining the appearance of the child. If it was as old as she said, it would not be covered with the blood that Karo believed would distinguish a baby born just a day earlier. Rabbi David ibn Zimra, a sixteenth century scholar also known as Radbaz, offered another explanation, proposing that Solomon was able to recognize a physical resemblance between the baby and its biological mother.

This tradition of trying to penetrate Solomon's reasoning continues into our era. My favorite example is an actual 1920s court case presided over by Judge Vincent Brennan, a former Republican congressman who likewise was adjudicating a custody dispute between two women vying for the same child, this time a mother and a foster mother, and he decided to try to resolve the case the way that Solomon had. Brennan could not threaten to kill the child, of course; instead, as he announced that the child would be sent to an orphanage rather than be given to either of the two women, he secretly captured the reactions of the two women with hidden cameras. After studying their responses in consultation with psychological experts, the judge awarded custody to the woman who showed "a much more biological emotional reaction"—crying, sobbing, lips quivering—rather than to the other woman, who stood expressionless. As many of us assume today, Brennan believed that the king solved the case through a clever ruse, the threat of taking the child from both of the women was a test of their maternal bond, and that was what he was trying to emulate with the help of modern technology and psychology.

It would seem a Solomonic outcome, except that the woman awarded custody was not the actual biological mother. One problem with Brennan's reasoning, apart from its indifference to the pain the women suffered from such an ordeal, was its assumption that the key to Solomon's judgment was the king's psychological insightfulness, his perception that one could ascertain the truth if one only knew how to interpret the mother's behavior correctly (even Freud, incidentally, tried his hand at analyzing Solomon's judgment in a work called *Group Psychology and the Analysis of the Ego*). But such a method, even if it could determine the better mother, cannot reveal the biological one. Modern-day advocates of adoption rightly contest the assumption that biological birth generates a unique emotional bond—adoptive parents can love their children much more deeply than the biological parents who give them up—and premodern interpreters also recognized that this was no fail-safe method for determining the true mother. Yohanan Alemanno, an early modern Jewish mystic who was famous as the teacher of the Renaissance scholar Pico della Mirandola and who authored a work on Solomon called *Hesheq Shlomo*, recalls cases when parents were prepared to see their children die or even to kill them themselves rather than betray a core principle or suffer humiliation. In other words, it was possible to imagine a motive that would lead the true mother to agree to her child's death; perhaps she was so proud or uncompromising that she was prepared to sacrifice her child rather than betray the truth. As any advocate of adoption would tell you, identifying the better parent is not the same as identifying the biological parent.

Brennan's effort to imitate Solomon's judgment was not only ridiculous—even at the time it was recognized as a shameless Hollywood-style publicity stunt—it missed its whole point. No subsequent judge could ever fully reproduce the king's judgment, no matter how much expertise he drew on, because what distinguished this case from all others was precisely that it reached a conclusion unreachable through observation or reasoned inference. In fact, what Brennan was unable to solve no subsequent jurist or theorist has been able to figure out either. It is not for lack of trying. Some economists and game theorists have tried to find a solution to what is known as King Solomon's Dilemma, the problem of how to fairly divide an indivisible good, but judging from some recent irresolvable cases—the question of who won the 2000 presidential election, for example—no one has figured out how to resolve this kind of dilemma. From Rabbi Karo to Judge Brennan, all these efforts to penetrate Solomon's judgment share the idea that Solomon used some clever but comprehensible method to solve his case, one that others could also adopt, and this is precisely the problem with them; by explaining Solomon's judgment, by figuring out how he did it, they robbed it of its extraordinariness, of what it is that elevated his wisdom above that of other great sages.

Reflecting on difficult child custody cases in particular, the social theorist Jon Elster concluded in his book *Solomonic Judgements* that the belief that such cases can somehow be solved rationally is itself irrational; tracking the outcomes of such cases reveals that flipping a coin to determine who gets the child is as effective as any of the methods that modern judges apply. Elster's conclusion is relevant for understanding the original story of Solomon's judgment. Not only does no rational solution to this kind of dilemma exist today, perhaps there never was a rational solution to it, with Solomon himself able to solve it only because he was not operating within the bounds of ordinary reasoning. The wisdom that was guiding his decision was not born of any explicable method, procedure, or ruse—that is, the kind of wisdom that a philosopher might achieve; in fact, the Bible places it in opposition to such wisdom, casting it as an unparalleled level of insight the likes of which no other sage had ever reached or would ever reach again. Every attempt to explain Solomon's judgment in light of ordinary rationality thus misses the mark because the defining characteristic of that judgment is precisely its difference from ordinary rationality: the ability it demonstrates to derive a truth that no human being, drawing on intelligence, skill, or experience, is able to ascertain.

What made Solomon's wisdom so special, in other words, was its superhuman character: it did not originate in his own mind but came to him through divine revelation, as a gift bestowed on him by God. Not long after he secured the throne, and shortly before the two mothers brought him their case, Solomon went up to a place called Gibeon, a few miles northwest of Jerusalem, to make a sacrifice of a thousand burnt offerings to the Lord. His choice of Gibeon to worship God is troubling. Why didn't he offer sacrifice in Jerusalem, the site chosen by God for such purposes and that he himself would make even more central by building a Temple there? The Chronicler was so disturbed by this that he felt moved to invent a fact not mentioned in Kings, that the king chose the site because the Tabernacle, the tent that Moses had constructed for the worship of God, was still there. In any case, while God may be a bit suspicious of Solomon for this reason, he does not seem too angry with him because that night he appears to him in the dream that we tried to analyze in chapter 3, the dream where he asks Solomon what he wants. We recall the wisdom of the young king's response; he seeks neither riches nor long life, nor the defeat of his enemies—the kinds of requests that most kings would have made under the circumstances—but rather an "understanding mind," the knowledge and judgment needed to help him govern his people. In response to this request God grants Solomon divine wisdom—not the political cunning he exhibits in 1 Kings 2, nor the psychological insight that Freud associated with him, nor any other species of human rationality, for that matter, but a supernatural wisdom surpassing that of humans because it came directly from God: "God gave Solomon very great wisdom, discernment, and broad understanding as vast as the sand on the seashore. Solomon's wisdom was greater than the wisdom of all the people of the east, and all the wisdom of Egypt. He was wiser than anyone else" (Heb 5: 9–11). The midrashic work *Pesikta de Rav Kahana*, an ancient collection of rabbinic homilies based on the Torah, explains that the wisdom of the east was horoscopes and bird augury; of Egypt, astrology. These were the methods by which the ancients penetrated beyond the visible world and saw into the future; the knowledge they revealed was also supposedly divine but even so it was still highly limited when compared with the wisdom of Solomon, based as it was on ambiguous, puzzling hints of which one might catch a glimpse in the movements of the heavens or birds in flight. This is not the kind of wisdom that God instilled in Solomon—his wisdom seems to have been greater, vaster, far more encompassing and penetrating, a wisdom that understood everything clearly, directly, all at once, in the way that God himself did.

What was it exactly that this wisdom revealed to Solomon? We can tell from the story of the two prostitutes that it must have included an ability to solve extremely difficult problems, but there are hints in 1 Kings that it encompassed much more. With a knowledge "as vast as the sands on the seashore," Solomon became a master of proverbs and songs, uttering them by the thousands, and he seems to have had an encyclopedic knowledge of the natural world as well, discoursing on all manner of plants and animals. Eventually, in fact, people came to believe that he knew everything there was to know—knowledge of practical subjects like how to heal disease or construct a building but also more abstruse subjects, such as the hidden architecture of the universe or the secret thoughts of God. In an age that has largely demystified the world, it is hard to fully appreciate what such understanding meant to earlier readers of Solomon's story. Knowing what God knew, having the key to the most mysterious aspects of life, meant that one never had to face the terror of the unknown or fall prey to duplicity. If knowledge is power, perfect knowledge meant absolute power, an ability to control the forces of nature, to manipulate human psychology, and even to predict what the future will bring. Such knowledge was thought to be so empowering, in fact, that it wasn't just scholars and philosophers who coveted it; emperors and sultans did as well.

All of which is to explain why the question we are posing here—what did Solomon know that the rest of us do not?—has tremendous existential implication, or at least it did before modernity deflated the value of wisdom. What was at stake in this question was an understanding not just of good governance or successful conflict resolution but of life itself and its most elusive mysteries—how to find love, how to be successful, what lies after death, what is the point of it all—and people felt that if they could answer it, if they could learn what Solomon knew, they could accomplish what he accomplished, exerting mastery over nature, overcoming fear, fulfilling every wish. Greek philosophy offered answers to some of these questions, but depending as it did on human perception rather than divine revelation, it was limited by the constraints of the senses, of human mobility, of mortality, and could thus only make educated guesses about those aspects of life that could not be observed directly. Solomon, by contrast, had penetrated those secrets, which is why the effort to understand what he understood became one of the great, if quixotic, intellectual quests of all time, obsessing not just biblical scholars but philosophers, magicians, mystics, explorers, even scientists.

To make progress in their quest for Solomonic knowledge, however, interpreters had to first overcome the limits of the biblical text. Kings and Chronicles do not reveal much about Solomon's wisdom. They praise its greatness, they quantify its benefits, but they never reveal its contents. Even the little information that is provided is more mystifying than illuminating. The text reports, "He uttered three thousand proverbs," but does this mean that his wisdom taught him how to compose proverbs, an art that requires great perspicacity and pithiness, or merely how to recite them in great numbers? The answer is unclear. We read that he was able to solve the difficult questions posed to him by the Queen of Sheba, but what were those questions, and how did he solve them? We aren't told. Before one can discover the secret of Solomon's wisdom, one must, paradoxically, act as if one already possesses such wisdom, seeking to penetrate hidden aspects of the text that lie beyond the reach of ordinary discernment.

Later chapters will track how interpreters tried to overcome this problem and will also attempt to discern some of the secrets buried in the text, but the gaps in our knowledge, as irresolvable as they may seem, do not pose our greatest interpretive challenge. Interpreters reading between the lines of the biblical story discovered something else hidden there as well, something sinister that emerges from Solomon's wisdom and that raised questions about whether it was worth pursuing after all. The insights that it revealed allowed Solomon to accomplish extraordinary things, to impose justice and peace, to acquire great wealth, to build the Temple, and yet he does not turn out to be such an admirable figure in the end, failing to live up to the destiny encoded into his name. Perfect wisdom should have protected him from such missteps—wisdom was supposed to lead to virtue and prosperity, not to sin and misfortune—and interpreters spent much effort trying to figure out what went wrong, but they faced a biblical text that merely hinted at answers, never revealing them in full. By reading between the lines, however, some discovered that the problem lay in Solomon's wisdom itself; as perfect as it was, there was something disturbing about it as well.

Intimations of wisdom's dark underside surface even in Solomon's most famous act of wisdom, the judgment recorded in 1 Kings 3, at least as this episode was read by the rabbis of the Talmudic age. One might have expected the rabbis, fascinated as they were with how to resolve difficult legal cases, to have been greater admirers of Solomon. Many were, equating his wisdom with the knowledge of the Torah that they themselves pursued, but not every sage was so impressed; some were actually extremely critical of him. We have already noted some rabbinic discontent with the way Solomon treated Joab, but that was supposed to have happened before the king acquired divine wisdom. Even more remarkably, rabbis exposed similar injustices in the trial of 1 Kings 3, which was supposed to be a demonstration of Solomon's wisdom.

Earlier interpreters were willing to gloss over the procedural flaws in the trial, the ways in which it violated Jewish law—an example is the Pompey painting, which adds two other judges to the scene in an apparent effort to align it with the law requiring three judges in a case like this—but not so the rabbis. Thus, the Babylonian Talmud, in tractate *Rosh Hashana* 21b, seems disturbed by the fact that he tried to resolve the case of the two prostitutes based on his own judgment rather than on the testimony of two witnesses as required by the Torah, and it also troubled the Talmudic sages that Solomon was willing to impose such a harsh judgment, ready and willing to cut a child in two in his quest for the truth. A rabbi named Yehuda was reportedly so upset by the order that he would have turned the tables on Solomon and imposed a death sentence on the king himself: "Had I been there, I would have strangled him."

What such readers discovered between the lines of the text, in other words, was a kind of counterhistory to the story that the Bible tells in an explicit way. On the surface, Solomon's wisdom seems to be nothing but a blessing, answering every question, solving every problem, bringing unbelievable good fortune to the king himself and creating an era of peace and prosperity the likes of which Israel had never known. Beneath this tale, however, the rabbis and other readers detected another, more disturbing story; even after he acquired divine wisdom, the king may not have been that different from the unscrupulously ambitious figure we reconstructed in the previous chapter—pitiless, presumptuous, playing the judge but a little too heedless of the limits that God had placed on human judgment. The explicit story is, of course, the more accessible and better remembered of the two—many readers of the biblical accounts never even suspect the presence of criticism smuggled into the narrative's praise of Solomon—but as we will see, the second story has long been a part of collective consciousness as well.

Not unlike Solomon himself, therefore, we find ourselves faced not with one account of what really happened but with different, contradictory understandings of the king's life that can be drawn from the account in Kings—positive and negative. Which of these reveals the true nature of Solomon, the explicit account of an extraordinary sage who knows the solution to every problem, or the between-the-lines story of a figure grown presumptuous and cruel under the influence of limitless knowledge? We cannot say because we lack Solomon's insight. When one views life without the benefit of divine wisdom, there is often no way to distinguish between fact and falsehood, and that is the predicament we find ourselves in as we wrestle with the spare, unverifiable testimony of Kings. The good news is that there is no child at stake, only our own compulsion to know hidden things, and that means that we can afford *not* to pass a final judgment on Solomon and his wisdom, attending to contradictory interpretations without ruling on which is more truthful and which less so. We will never reach a definitive understanding of the king's life in this way, I admit, but that is a level of understanding reserved for God and Solomon in any case, and hearing both sides without needing to judge between them may yet reveal another kind of wisdom, wisdom that is tentative, equivocal, even self-contradictory, but that also happens to be within reach of those without the wisdom of God to guide them.

5

Sacred Books, Satanic Verses

ACCORDING TO I KINGS 5:13, which provides a description of Solomon's wisdom, the king's wisdom gave him the ability to speak "about beasts and fowl, creeping things and fish." The text is probably referring to Solomon's ability to converse about the natural world, or maybe about his skill at using animals as illustrations—as Aesop was famous for doing—but through a slight reinterpretation of the Hebrew it gave rise to a legend that Solomon knew how to talk to the animals, that he could speak *to* the beasts and fowl. Where other people heard only meaningless squeaks and squawks, bellows and roars, the king could recognize the ant's cry for help as he scrambled to escape his footfalls, the arrogance of the crowing rooster, and the desperate pleas of a cow about to be slaughtered.

Freud was not the only scientist to look to this story as a metaphor for his quest for hidden knowledge. In 1949, the Austrian zoologist Konrad Lorenz, famous for his efforts to explain the instinctive behavior of animals, published a book that claimed to divulge King Solomon's secret. After years of animal research, Lorenz boasted that he too had penetrated the mysterious ways in which animals communicated with one another. His methods for reconstructing the knowledge of Solomon were modern, but the ambition that drove him to achieve the kind of extraordinary insight that Solomon possessed was ancient.

How did it come about that scientists like Lorenz—or Freud, for that matter—looked to Solomon as a scientific forebear? The answer spans at least the last two thousand years of intellectual history. Already in the first century, the historian Josephus tells us that he once met a man named Eleazar who claimed to be schooled in the esoteric knowledge of Solomon, magical and exorcistic knowledge that gave Eleazar the power to control demons and drive them out of the people whom they possessed. Eleazar derived this power by repeating certain incantations that Solomon composed, but Josephus also mentions that the magician used a ring that derived its curative effects from a special root hidden under its seal that had been prescribed by Solomon. Josephus's reference to this ring might be what gave rise to the legendary Ring of Solomon known from later rabbinic, Christian, and Muslim sources, thought to derive its power from the secret name of God inscribed on its seal. Solomon is supposed to have used the ring to perform marvelous feats, to summon the winds to lift him aloft, and to understand the animals, which is why Lorenz used it as the title of his book *King Solomon's Ring*.

As the Middle Ages gave way to modernity, and as magic evolved into science, Solomon underwent a corresponding transmutation from a sorcerer into a scientist. The most influential invocation of Solomon in this regard was that of the seventeenth century natural philosopher Francis Bacon in his work *The New Atlantis*, an account of a fictional journey to a mythical island that Bacon used to work out his vision of scientific inquiry. The island that Bacon describes in this work, loosely based on the islands discovered in the New World and South Pacific by Columbus and other explorers, was ruled by a king named Solamona—not our Solomon but a suspiciously similar figure, whose greatest accomplishment is the establishment of Solamona's House, which seems modeled on the Temple but was really a kind of scientific institute, a society dedicated to acquiring the knowledge of the natural world that Solomon was thought to have possessed. Solamona's House was a fictional vision of what the scientific enterprise should look like, but it went on to serve as a model for real-life scientific societies like the Royal Society in London, the Ashmolean Museum in Oxford, and the College of Physicians in London, the latter declared by the Royal physician Walter Charleton to be "Solomon's House in reality." Lorenz was being playful in his reference to Solomon, but the title articulates one of the earliest motives for scientific investigation—an aspiration to understand the world as deeply as Solomon did.

But how could later scholars hope to know what Solomon knew when Solomon's wisdom was supposed to be unique? When God revealed himself to the king in the dream at Gibeon, he seemed to say that he was giving the king wisdom and understanding far greater than that of any other mortal: "No one like you has been before you, and no one like you shall arise after you" (1 Kings 3:12). In contrast to all the sages who came after him, his insights arose not from study, reflection, or observation but from a miracle, an extraordinary act of divine intervention that made it possible for him to grasp what no mortal should ever have been able to know. The idea that Solomon's wisdom was irreproducible did not sit well with the insatiably curious, however—the scholars, philosophers, and scientists of later ages who could not achieve direct access to divine knowledge in the way that Solomon did, but who were no less intellectually ambitious. They wanted to know what the king knew, the cryptic language of animals and other secrets, and they had reason to think it possible to do so, for tradition held that the king had left behind a record of his wisdom, books that disclosed the secrets that he knew.

These writings are nowhere mentioned in 1 Kings. It reports that Solomon uttered three thousand proverbs and 1,005 songs but nowhere suggests that these or any other of the king's insights were written down. Solomonic writings are, of course, to be found elsewhere in the Hebrew Bible, however—in the books of Proverbs, the Song of Songs, and Ecclesiastes. According to critical scholarship, none of these works is a genuine Solomonic composition. Proverbs seems to have been compiled in the time of King Hezekiah or later, while the Song of Songs and Ecclesiastes feature linguistic features that date them to a still later age, the period of Persian rule that followed a few decades after the destruction of Solomon's Temple in 586 B.C.E. But this is to read these texts as ordinary human compositions when, according to early Jews and Christians, that is precisely how one should *not* read them. "Had Solomon composed them out of his own mind, it would have been incumbent on you to incline your ear and listen to them," noted one rabbi, "all the more then since he composed them in the holy spirit" (*Song of Songs Rabbah* 1,8). Jewish and Christian Bibles include these works because they were seen as the work not of the human intellect alone but of divinely inspired prophecy.

If we read these books as a record of Solomon's divine wisdom, what do we learn? For early Jews and Christians, they were a key to understanding scripture itself. One of the early interpreters to read the works of Solomon in this way, the Christian mystic Origen of Alexandria, actually uses the key as a metaphor for the kind of interpretation we have in mind. Origen claimed to have learned from a Jewish teacher that scripture was like a house with many doors. Each door had a key lying before it, but the keys had been confused and it took great effort to match each key to the correct door. That was the secret to understanding the true meaning of scripture, Origen's Jewish teacher taught him—how to use one biblical passage to unlock the secrets of another. For both early Jews and Christians the writings of Solomon functioned in this way, helping to reveal the hidden significance of other scriptural texts. As the rabbis put it, "Till Solomon arose no one was able to understand properly the words of the Torah, but as soon as Solomon arose, all began to comprehend the Torah" (*Song of Songs Rabbah* 1,8).

If you pick up a Bible yourself, and skim through Proverbs, the Song of Songs, and Ecclesiastes, you will find that none of them seems to reveal any deep insights into the Bible's meaning. What one finds in Proverbs, for example, is a collection of very pragmatic teachings, practical advice about how to stay out of trouble and live a long and prosperous life, and its conception of wisdom does not seem especially abstruse or mystical. But that is because we are reading these verses in a way that is very different from the kind of interpretation practiced by early biblical readers like the rabbis. In their view, the proverbs of Solomon were not proverbs in our sense of that genre, brief and catchy observations (in Miguel de Cervantes' aptly pithy definition, a proverb is a short sentence based on a lifetime of experience). Rather, as we have noted, they were what we would call a parable or allegory, teachings that cloak their point in the guise of a story or image. In the rabbinic understanding, the mashal was a good description of Solomon's entire literary corpus: some of his writing reflected his own personal experiences, but for the most part it was a kind of encrypted commentary on the Torah, helping to unveil meanings that would otherwise be indiscernible.

The *Song of Songs Rabbah*, a collection of rabbinic interpretations that read the Song of Songs as an allegorical commentary on the Sinai story, makes this point by means of a parable of its own:

> You find that until Solomon came there was no parable (*mashal*, translated as parable here but the same word underlying the Hebrew for Proverbs, *Mishlei*). Said Rabbi Nahman: Imagine a large palace with many doors, so that whoever entered could not find his way back to the door, till one clever person came and took a coil of string and hung it up on the way to the door, so that all went in and out by means of the coil. So until Solomon arose no one was able to grasp the words of Torah, but as soon as Solomon arose all began to comprehend the Torah.

Nahman's parable calls to mind Origen's comparison of scripture to a palace with many doors (it is distinctly possible that the Jewish teacher from whom Origen learned this metaphor was a rabbi like Nahman), and it ascribes to Solomon's parables a similar keylike role; the purpose of Solomon's writings, Nahman was suggesting, was to decode the Bible, to help others to penetrate the meaning concealed beneath its surface.

This by itself would have made Solomon's literary legacy an immense one, but it was just the tip of the iceberg. As both Jews and Christians also recognized, Solomon's wisdom was not limited to the Torah; it encompassed the entirety of reality, including those aspects of existence that were beyond human perception—the hidden forces of nature, the inner workings of the human body, the mystery of the future—and he was thought to have recorded this knowledge as well. This aspect of Solomon's wisdom is not as familiar as the kind recorded in Proverbs and Ecclesiastes. It was written in books that were not included in the Bible that Jews and many Protestants read, books that, with a few exceptions, have been lost over the centuries. They were once the object of intense curiosity, however. With the exceptions of the philosopher Aristotle and the divine Egyptian sage Hermes Trismegistus, in fact, the writings of no ancient wise man were thought to reveal more about the nature of existence than the books Solomon left behind.

The best known of these extrabiblical writings is the *Wisdom of Solomon*, part of the Catholic and Orthodox Christian biblical canons, which illumines that most impenetrable of secrets—the fate of people after they die. But the *Wisdom of Solomon* is just one of scores of works attributed to King Solomon: there are the *Psalms of Solomon*, eighteen extrabiblical psalms that include prophecies of the messianic age; the *Odes of Solomon*, another collection of Solomonic hymns; the *Testament of Solomon*, and even more obscure writings with titles like the *Hygromanteia of Solomon*, purportedly the instructions of Solomon to his son Rehoboam. The biblical writings of Solomon are but a fraction of his oeuvre: the Jewish mystic Yohanan Alemanno knew of at least thirty extracanonical works composed by Solomon, and there were probably many more than that.

Some of these writings record magical secrets—how to conjure demons, turn lead into gold, become invisible, and perform other supernatural feats. The Solomon of the Bible is no wizard, but interpreters detected there allusions to his magical expertise, as in 1 Kings 5:18 (5:4 in some English translations): "Now the Lord has given me rest all around: there is no adversary or misfortune." On the surface, the verse has nothing to do with magic, but the words translated here as "adversary" and "misfortune," *satan* and *pega ra*, can also be read as "Satan" and "evil spirit," and such a reading—a quite plausible rendering for ancient and medieval readers obsessed with the role of demonic forces in their lives—makes Solomon into a master sorcerer. The king was thought to have recorded his knowledge of the demonic realm, along with love potions and other magical secrets in books known as *grimoires*, magical textbooks like the *Ars Notoria*, a collection of magical prayers, diagrams, and rituals; or the *Almandel* (derived from the Arabic *al-mudhil*, "the secret revealer"), which teaches how to converse with angels.

Other Solomonic books disclose what we would call scientific knowledge. To this day, the king enjoys a reputation as a master herbalist—in Jamaica he is credited with discovering marijuana, known there as the "Wisdom Weed"—and this tradition goes back to the first part of the verse with which we began this chapter, 1 Kings 5:13: "He spoke about trees ranging from the cedars of Lebanon to the hyssop that grows out of the wall . . . ," understood to mean that Solomon delivered learned discourses on botany, pharmacology, and medicine. Many sources credit Solomon with medical or biological writings, including Bacon, who refers to such a writing in the *New Atlantis* as a "Natural History, which [Solomon] wrote of all Plants from the Cedars of Libanus, to the Mosse that growth out of the Wall; And of all things that haue Life and Motion." Other scientific works attributed to Solomon include treatises on mathematics, astronomy, and alchemy.

What unites all the various kinds of writings attributed to Solomon, transcending the boundary between magic, mysticism, and science that we impose today, is their engagement with powers and principles at work in the universe that lie beyond the sense perception of ordinary humans. The Torah has its manifest meaning, the stories and laws that any child can understand, but beneath its surface lie hidden levels of meaning, invisible lessons and insights that became comprehensible only when Solomon wrote *meshalim* to help explain them. In a similar way, the king revealed the hidden subtext of the natural world—the invisible forces at work in the blowing of the wind and the movements of the stars, the untapped energy concealed within minerals and plants, the miraculously intricate, mysteriously self-forming machinery of the human body. The image of the key often comes up in connection to Solomon as a metaphor for his wisdom, as in the title of works like the *Key of Solomon*, another magical treatise, and with good reason. There was so much to be gained by learning the secrets of nature, not just knowledge but health and power, but to premodern scholars it was as if this knowledge had been locked away behind a door they simply could not open, referring to things that, in an age before microscopes and X-rays, were impossible to see directly or to penetrate. This is what made Solomon's writings so fascinating for those who would gain access to these secrets; they unlocked the door.

But this is also what made these writings very dangerous. Solomon has the distinction of being one of the few authors in history to have had his writings both canonized and censored. Three of his books made it into the Bible, but most were excluded, some were even banned, and even his biblical writings were controversial—some ancient rabbis thought that even they should not be included in the canon. Their authenticity probably wasn't the problem: a few premodern scholars had their doubts—Jerome questioned the Solomonic authorship of the *Wisdom of Solomon*, for example—but such doubts did not prevail until modernity and the onset of critical scholarship. What seems to have made them problematic in the premodern period was their disclosure of secret knowledge—knowledge, it was assumed, that must have been hidden for a reason.

Christian authorities like Saint Augustine condemned the investigation of the natural world as a vice or sin, a distraction from what was really important (*Confessions* 10.35), and some rabbinic authorities, sharing this sense that humans weren't meant to know what they couldn't see, also discouraged the investigation of metaphysical questions (metaphysics in the Aristotelian definition is the investigation of aspects of experience that lie beyond sense perception). The influence of this view did much to suppress interest in Christian Europe in the scientific and magical teachings that the Middle Ages inherited from antiquity, leaving them to the Islamic world, but then there was the counterexample of Solomon. Didn't his writings show that that the investigation of life's mysteries could be consistent with religious piety? Early scientists like Francis Bacon were interested in Solomon for precisely this reason—his example seemed to legitimize scientific investigation—but others drew a different conclusion: Solomon learned more than God wanted to reveal, discovering knowledge that was dangerous for humans to possess, and his magical/scientific writings, to the extent they disclosed that knowledge, were dangerous too and for that reason had not been preserved in the Bible.

Thus arose a tradition attested in both Jewish and Christian sources that some of Solomon's writings didn't appear in the Bible not because they were considered pseudepigrapha but because they had been suppressed by authorities concerned that they revealed too much. In one tradition, the offending book was a collection of remedies, and King Hezekiah did away with it, the story goes, when he saw that the people had grown to depend on it rather than turn to God for healing. He did not question the book's authenticity or its efficacy. To the contrary, it was its efficacy that disturbed him; the medical knowledge that Solomon disclosed worked so well that it lulled the people into believing they no longer needed God. In another tradition preserved in out-of-the-way Christian sources, Solomon himself anticipates Hezekiah's concern. Realizing that his wisdom could lead others to doubt God, he orders his writings to be burned.

Both stories are legends, attempts to explain why certain books attributed to Solomon were excluded from the Bible, but they may also reflect what did in fact happen to some of Solomon's extrabiblical writings during the Middle Ages. Medieval scholars like Roger Bacon and Albertus Magnus condemned certain Solomon writings as false and evil—one scholar even urged Christians not to mention Solomonic books like the

Almandel—and at least one book of Solomonic magic was put to fire in Paris in 1323. The impulse to suppress Solomon's writings was a very real one

But how could the writings of Solomon have produced such divergent responses? The biblical writings attributed to the king, seen as a record of divine wisdom, inspired reverence: people looked to them for understanding and guidance. Many of Solomon's extrabiblical writing recorded a very different kind of wisdom, the forbidden knowledge associated with sorcery and pagan divination, and they provoked a very different response—marginalization, condemnation, even censorship. How could the saintly author responsible for the pious tomes of Proverbs and the Song of Songs have also written treatises on black magic?

The answer that some sources suggest is that Solomon was privy to two kinds of otherworldly wisdom. The wisdom that God bestowed on the king, the wisdom recorded in Proverbs, Song of Songs, and Ecclesiastes, offered insight into the secrets of Torah, but it did not seek to disclose forbidden knowledge—the knowledge of magical and scientific subjects. That other kind of wisdom came from a different source, the same source that revealed wisdom to Eve. God was not the source of his wisdom; Solomon had acquired it from other ungodly sources—this or that demon, or the Devil himself—and doing so proved to be the king's downfall.

One version of this tradition is inspired by a story that appears in the Babylonian Talmud, in tractate *Gittin* 67–68, and concerns a devil named Asmodeus—in rabbinic lore, the king of the demons. Asmodeus was known for his ability to foresee disastrous events, but according to the Talmud he also possessed a secret that Solomon needed to enable him to complete the Temple. To finish the Temple, the king had to overcome the challenge of how to fit its stones into place without violating the Torah's command against using iron tools in the building of the sanctuary. The only way to do so was to enlist the power of a special worm, called the shamir, that was able to cut into any substance, but only Asmodeus knew where to find the worm, and so Solomon set out to capture the demon. The king, of course, was very clever—he got Asmodeus drunk and imprisoned him with a ring and chain inscribed with the divine name—but the demon proved even more cunning, for it eventually tricked Solomon into setting him free. Liberated from Solomon's control, he drove the king away, assumed his form, and took his place, and it was during this period, according to a medieval elaboration of this story, that Asmodeus wrote certain magic spells and left them under Solomon's throne, writings preserved in a text referred to in Jewish medieval sources as the book of Asmodeus. Some of Solomon's writings were suspect, this tradition suggests, because they were the work of the devil himself.

If this part of Solomon's story seems at all familiar, it may be because it is a distant ancestor of our own culture's ambivalence about the pursuit of knowledge. One of the great parables for that ambivalence is the legend of Dr. Faust, which was itself the inspiration for Frankenstein and other stories of scientists destroyed by the secrets that they learn. Faust was a German magician who made a compact with a devil named Mephistopheles, selling his soul for magical knowledge. His story is a kind of retelling of the story of Solomon's dealings with Asmodeus, drawing on legends like the rabbinic story recounted above, with Mephistopheles giving Faust a book of spells that reminds one of the book of Asmodeus. It is this book that is the source of Faust's magical power, and for twenty-four years he draws on what he learns from it to perform various wonders. Finally, though, it comes time for Faust to die and for Mephistopheles to take him off to hell per their agreement, and it is at that moment that the magician confronts the cost of his secret knowledge and repents of his learning. As the devil comes for him, Faust decrees, "I will burn my books"—an echo of Solomon's resolve to burn his books.

In the end, it is not censorship that has concealed most of the so-called writings of Solomon but disinterest. Many of these writings have disappeared not because they were actively censored for their heretical content but because people simply stopped reading them once they found other ways of revealing reality's hidden dimensions, ways that do not rely on magic rings, demonic informants, or ancient books. But the dilemma that Solomon's writings pose has not disappeared. The desire that produced so many of these writings, the ambition to penetrate the world's secrets, still persists, finding new ways to satisfy humanity's craving for knowledge even as it raises the same moral questions that Solomon's extrabiblical writings did for earlier ages: Can one know too much about the world? Are certain kinds of knowledge too dangerous to pursue?

Of course, we are much more sympathetic to scientific inquiry than medieval religious authorities were, but even we can have second thoughts about pursuing certain kinds of knowledge. Consider Lorenz's book *King Solomon's Ring*. We began this chapter by noting how Solomon's wisdom inspired Lorenz's groundbreaking research into the animal world. As it happens, however, much of it was first published during the Nazi period, and its science is implicated in the evils of that era. Lorenz himself was a member of the Nazi Party, and his research on animals probably garnered Nazi support because of its possible implications for the movement's racial theories. Lorenz's account is a fascinating revelation of nature's secrets, but such knowledge, it turns out, is regrettable, emerging from a deal with the devil. In medieval times, the magic manuals and protoscientific treatises attributed to Solomon confronted medieval authorities with a similar dilemma: should they allow these books to reveal their secrets, or uphold the moral boundaries which separate human understanding from the realm of demons?

As Roger Shattuck has shown in his book *Forbidden Knowledge*, prior to the modern world people had a clear sense that there were certain things they were not supposed to know because such transgressive understanding would lead them astray or violate the limits that God imposed on his creatures. We've lost that sense in the modern world. Our motto is not "Be lowly wise" (Milton, from his retelling of the Garden of Eden story in *Paradise Lost*) but the philosopher Kant's injunction "Dare to know." The religious institutions that once reined in curiosity have lost their authority in Western secular culture. It is now widely assumed that the pursuit of wisdom should be limitless.

But even today, the fear that one can learn too much persists, not just for religious opponents of science but also now for its advocates. We who live today make movies about robots turning against their masters, and we have nightmares about genetic science yielding mutants and monsters—all ways of expressing the worry that the pursuit of science is like letting an evil genie out of its bottle. That too is a legend that can be traced back to Solomon, and more specifically to the Talmudic story of Solomon and Asmodeus, a story we tell over and over again, long after its Talmudic antecedents have been forgotten, because it expresses a fear that has been rekindled by the overreaching of scientific curiosity. As ancient as Solomon's story is, it has gained new relevance as a parable of curiosity unleashed, a warning that the desire for limitless understanding, even in the canonized form of scientific inquiry, has something demonic written into it.

6

The King of Kings

WISDOM AS IT WAS UNDERSTOOD in the world that Solomon inhabited encompassed a wide range of knowledge and skills, including not just the ability to judge difficult cases but also what we would call medicine, art, and rhetoric. If there is a common denominator that unites all these skills, it is the ability to order shapeless stuff into well-designed arrangements— to restore the balance of the body, to turn formless stone or wood into well-crafted works of art, to bring sounds together into a compact, catchy proverb. This seems to be the essential power that Solomon acquires from God's gift of wisdom—the ability to impose balance, harmony, order.

The template for Solomon's conduct as a ruler was God's creation of the universe, which seemed to the ancients to adhere to an intricately designed, carefully patterned blueprint. According to the book of Proverbs, in fact, it was wisdom itself, imagined as a woman, who created this design: "When [God] established the heavens, I [Wisdom] was there, when he inscribed a circle on the face of the deep, when he fortified the skies above, when he reinforced the fountains of the deep, when he imposed on the sea its limit, so that the waters might not violate his word, when he marked out the foundations of the earth, I was with him, as an architect" (Proverbs 8:27–30). God's creation as described here is an act of putting the elements in their place, and Wisdom's role is to serve as architect or draftsman, drawing up the plans that determine what goes where. To possess wisdom is to grasp this design, to recognize how order can emerge from chaos, and to emulate it in one's own acts of creation.

Since we were not present at creation, we cannot understand its design ourselves, but God did share this knowledge with Solomon, and it helps to explain his genius for putting things in order. The king is the first to consolidate Israel's warring tribes into a single, well-organized kingdom, a feat that even Moses and David had a difficult time accomplishing. What allows him to do this, it seems, is the same kind of organizational skill that Wisdom uses to organize the world. Just as God divides a chaotic and conflict-ridden reality into distinct realms—the deep, the sky, water, and earth—Solomon divides his kingdom into districts, one for each tribe, then divides their responsibilities according to the twelve months of the year, each tribe given the responsibility to provide one month of provisions for the king. Introducing clear distinctions, then making sure the parts work together as part of a coordinated whole, Solomon creates a kingdom that mirrors the stability and equilibrium of the cosmos, and the correspondence is no coincidence: each is guided by wisdom.

The same organizational genius is reflected in another of Solomon's great accomplishments as king—his efforts as a builder. Building and wisdom are closely associated in the Bible and ancient Near Eastern literature. Ancient kings known for their wisdom, rulers like Hammurabi, displayed that wisdom not just by executing justice but also by building, and many ancient Near Eastern inscriptions attest to the idea that the greatest of buildings—the temple or the palace—required the wisdom of the gods themselves to complete, the same wisdom that the gods used to design the world. The wisdom that God gave to Solomon seems to have made him a master builder. It is really he, much more than David, who builds up Jerusalem into the sacred site that it is for Jews, Christians, and Muslims to this day by building a temple there that mirrored the design of the Garden of Eden, and his construction projects were by no means limited to that city as they included fortification of the cities of Hazor, Megiddo, Gezer; the building of new towns to house his chariots and cavalry; and a fleet of ships docked in the southern port-town of Ezion-geber. Solomon didn't design these buildings himself—he relied on Phoenician artisans—but it was he who marshaled the resources and workers necessary to undertake these projects, feats that reflected the same organizational genius that made him such a great administrator.

Solomon is so successful as a ruler that he wins the respect of all his peers, the kings of the earth, who come from every direction to hear his wisdom and honor him with gifts. He was what was known in later periods as the king of kings, not just a great king but a supreme ruler with power over all other earthly powers: "Solomon ruled over all the kingdoms from the Euphrates to the land of the Philistines, even to the border of Egypt; they brought gifts and served Solomon all the days of his life" (1 Kings 5:1; in some translations, 4:21).

No wonder, then, that so many later kings would look to Solomon as the paragon of royal power. Already in antiquity, Solomon was viewed as the exemplary king, someone to whom other kings should look to understand how to rule well. An apocryphal text known as the *Wisdom of Solomon*, attributed to the king but probably really composed in the second or first century B.C.E., purports to be a teaching addressed to the "rulers of the earth," as if Solomon were trying to instruct them in how to be wise like him. A few centuries later, the image of Solomon as an exemplary ruler shaped the New Testament's portrait of Jesus as a "king of kings." One associates Jesus with David because he was known as the "Son of David," but actually that title was one of a number of traits he shares in common with Solomon, who in this period was known as the ultimate peacemaker, a skilled composer of parables, and a master exorcist. The resemblance was not a coincidence. By this period, Solomon had already emerged as the ideal ruler in Jewish tradition, and the Solomonic traits ascribed to Jesus were the Gospels' way of signaling that he was this kind of ruler, or rather a new and improved version since, as Jesus is said to have told the scribes and Pharisees of his day, "Something greater than Solomon is here" (Matthew 12:42). Later Jewish would-be messiahs would also identify with Solomon. One messianic pretender from sixteenth century Portugal, Diogo Pires, went so far as to change his name to *Shlomo Molko*. In the next century, the greatest of failed messiahs, Sabbatai Zvi, called himself King Solomon as well. It is even conceivable that Gershom Scholem, who before he became the great scholar of Jewish messianism briefly fancied himself as the messiah, also saw himself in Solomon, since he comments in his diary on the messianic significance of his name, Scholem, from the same root as "Shlomo."

By the end of antiquity, Solomon had become the model not just of messianic rule but of temporal, earthly rule as well, imitated by both Christian and Islamic rulers seeking to cast themselves as a king to whom the whole world should submit. The most famous example from the Islamic world is the Ottoman ruler Suleiman the "Magnificent," who emulated the king not just in name (Suleiman is Arabic for Solomon) but also in deed, rebuilding Jerusalem and promoting justice throughout his realm. An example from the Christian world is James I, sponsor of the King James, or the "Authorized," Bible, who was eulogized at his funeral as "Great Britain's Salomon"—a lover of peace, justice, and learning. These are but two examples of a long list of Solomonic rulers that include the Byzantine emperors who ruled the Christian Roman Empire, Muslim rulers of Persia and India, and Catholic kings of Europe. Such figures have not fared well in our own age. Haile Selassie, the descendant of Solomon according to Ethiopian tradition, died under suspicious circumstances in 1975, ending one line of Solomonic rule, while the Iranian revolution, which unseated the shah of Iran from a peacock throne inspired by that of Solomon, ended another. But even today, there are rulers who identify themselves with Solomon. When the next monarch of Britain is crowned, for instance, he will be sitting on a throne, King Edward's Chair, modeled on Solomon's throne, his coronation patterned on the anointment ritual performed on the biblical king by the priest Zadok.

As this example suggests, the symbol of Solomonic rule is a special kind of throne, and by sitting on it a ruler showed himself (or herself, in the case of rulers like Queen Elizabeth) to be a similar kind of sovereign. According to 1 Kings 10:20, the throne was supposedly unique—"nothing like it was made in any kingdom"—but it was nonetheless something that later kings tried to emulate by following what few details are provided in the biblical text, which notes, for example, that the throne was covered in gold and flanked by lions on either side, and was mounted by way of six steps, each the resting place for two additional lions. The best-known example is the throne of Solomon fashioned for the kings of the Byzantine Empire, arguably the most sophisticated automated contraption of the premodern world. According to Jewish legend, Solomon's throne would literally come alive whenever the king sat on it— the golden lions sitting on each of its steps would begin roaring, other gilded beasts would begin to move, eagles would descend to place the crown on his head, songbirds would begin to sing. The throne could also rotate and even take flight. Some sources suggest it was an imitation of the heavenly throne, the throne from which God ruled the world, and its nature symbolism—the animals and plants that adorned the throne—was meant to suggest the power of a cosmocrat, a ruler who governs the entire universe and all its inhabitants. In an effort to claim this kind of power, the kings of Byzantium had their artisans reproduce the wonders of Solomon's throne, relying on some kind of hydraulic system to animate the beasts and trees that flanked the throne, simulate the sound of roaring lions and singing birds, and allow the throne to be raised or lowered automatically. The throne deeply impressed visitors like Liutprand of Cremona, an Italian bishop who visited Constantinople in 949 and sent a description back to Europe, and it may have inspired kings throughout both Christendom and the Islamic world to produce replicas on which they themselves could sit.

The effort to reproduce Solomon's throne symbolizes a larger ambition of many Christian and Muslim rulers—to be the kind of king that Solomon was. Earlier Jewish rulers like Herod the Great might have harbored Solomonic ambitions, but they never found themselves ruling a world empire in the way that later Christian and Muslim kings did. For guidance these rulers turned back to the Bible's greatest kings—to David, of course, but also to Solomon, who came to be seen not just as an Israelite ruler but as a cosmocrat. There did exist ancient precedent for how to rule wisely—the philosopher-king described in Plato's *Republic*—but Solomon had an advantage over such a figure, at least from the perspective of Jews, Christians, and Muslims; the latter was the idea of a pagan thinker, while Solomon was a pious believer whom God himself appointed to be king. While the philosopher-king exerted an important influence as a political ideal in medieval and early modern times, in Judaism, Christianity, and Islam that ideal was fused into the figure of Solomon, who thus became the exemplum of how to rule well.

But this approach to Solomon depends on a particular interpretation of the biblical text, one that assumes that it is possible to figure out what made him such a great king, and not everyone was convinced that it was possible to discover the secrets of his rule. Another Jewish legend, this one preserved in an Aramaic translation of the book of Esther, recounts how a number of kings tried to sit on Solomon's throne, only to fail. First came the mighty Nebuchadnezzar, who captured the throne during his conquest of Jerusalem. He knew that Solomon had only to alight the first step and the golden lions seated on its steps would lift him up to the throne's lofty seat. But when Nebuchadnezzar placed his foot on the first step, the lion stationed there stretched out its paw and struck his foot so hard that he was left with a limp for the rest of his life. The throne passed to other kingdoms, to Egypt and Greece, and one after another their rulers made their own attempts to sit on the throne, only to be rebuffed. Only the kings of Persia, who helped restore Solomon's Temple, seem to have been permitted to take their seats on Solomon's throne, but even their success isn't clear. According to another Jewish source, the throne rejected the Persians too (*Esther Rabbah* 1.2, 12).

Such stories, composed by Jews living under Byzantine or Muslim rulers, were a kind of protest against the Solomonic pretensions of these rulers, mocking their efforts to replicate his greatness, but they also reflected a careful reading of the biblical text, or at least a particular version of the biblical text. In 1 Kings 3:13, God says to Solomon, "No other king shall be like you." The Masoretic text adds, "all the days of your life," confining Solomon's unique status to his own day, but other versions of the biblical text—versions that would have been read by those who did not know the original Hebrew—omit that phrase, and without it the verse seems to claim that no other king, present or future, would ever be able to compare to Solomon. It might be possible for other rulers to imitate the king in a superficial way, to copy his throne or build an imitation temple, but the wisdom that makes Solomon such a great ruler, this passage suggests, was exceptional, a gift bestowed on Solomon alone.

This way of reading the Bible inspired its own important political tradition—an antimonarchic tradition that used Solomon's uniqueness to underscore the deficiencies of all other kings. Critics of monarchy like Isaac Abravanel, the great fifteenth century Spanish-Jewish scholar who was once accused of plotting against the king of Portugal, and the seventeenth century radically minded pastor Fredrik van Leenhof, an early modern democratic theorist who produced two treatises on Solomon to advance his republican views, made much of how exceptional he was, accentuating the contrasts between his enlightened rule and the corruption and mediocrity of other kings not simply to honor Solomon but also to discredit the monarchs of their own day.

We now know, thanks to the discovery of other ancient Near Eastern kingdoms, that Solomon, assuming he existed, probably was not that unique a ruler. Consider, for example, the case of Azitiwada, a Phoenician king who ruled two centuries after Solomon. In 1946–47, an inscription from Azitiwada's reign was discovered in the ancient fort of Karatepe in what is now southeastern Turkey but which was once, three millennia ago, within the orbit of Phoenician culture, a variant of the same culture that existed in the land of Canaan in the centuries before Solomon. The longest known document written in Phoenician, the Karatepe inscription suggests that Solomon may not have been as unparalleled as Kings seems to suggest—or rather, to be more precise, that other kings of the era claimed to be comparably extraordinary:

> I am Azitiwada, blessed of Baal, servant of Baal, exalted by Awarku, king of the Danunians. Baal made me a father and a mother to the Danunians: I gave life to the Danunians: I expanded the land of the plain of Adana from east to west. In my days, the Danunians had every pleasant thing, plentiful and fine food, and I filled the granaries [or temples] of Pahar. I added horse upon horse, shield upon shield; army upon army thanks to Baal and the gods, and I decimated dissenters, I drove out all the evil that was in the land . . . and I made peace with every king, *and indeed every king esteemed me as a father for my righteousness and my wisdom.*

The public career of this king, described here by Azitiwada himself, is remarkably similar to that of Solomon. Appointed to the role of king by a god (in this case Baal, the head of the Canaanite/Phoenician pantheon), he expands the borders of his kingdom, increases the prosperity of his people, overcomes all opposition, undertakes great construction projects, acquires many horses, and makes peace with other kings—a résumé that precisely corresponds to the list of accomplishments attributed to Solomon in 1 Kings 3–10. Azitiwada even mirrors Solomon's most celebrated trait, earning the admiration of all his fellow kings for his righteousness and wisdom.

Phoenician culture was very closely related to that of ancient Israel—the two cultures bordered one another, their languages were virtually identical, and we know from 1 Kings that Solomon in particular enjoyed a close relationship with a Phoenician king, Hiram of Tyre, relying on his craftsman to help design the Temple. It seems likely, therefore, that the parallels noted above are no coincidence; the author of the biblical account seems to have been drawing on the same repertoire of rhetorical clichés that Phoenician scribes used to depict their kings, including the depiction of the king as the ultimate sage, wiser, more righteous and more just than everyone else.

In fact, the image of the king as a sage was a widespread one in the ancient world. Americans today tend to be suspicious of rulers who come across as smarter than the rest of us—as a colleague noted, whenever President Obama is described as "professorial," that usually isn't meant as a compliment—but the sage king was a much admired figure in the ancient world. Some of the greatest kings of antiquity—Hammurabi, the Babylonian lawgiver, or Assurbanipal, the learned scholar-king of Assyria—fashioned themselves as wise figures elevated above other mortals by their access to the secrets of the cosmos. The biblical description of Solomon reflects this trope; it turns out that even his much admired wisdom, the very trait that supposedly distinguishes him as a king, is a trait he shares with other rulers from the era.

All this would seem to undercut the Bible's claim that Solomon was unlike any other king, but that description, it needs to be noted, was referring to the king's wealth and fame and need not be extended to other aspects of his rule. Elsewhere in Kings, in fact, there are intimations that Solomon may not have been as unique a ruler as he was later perceived to be, that he does in fact bear a resemblance to other kings.

One of these intimations appears much earlier in the biblical text, long before the birth of Solomon, even before Israel's first king Saul. For many centuries, since the death of Joshua, the Israelites had been led by judges, charismatic rulers, usually military leaders, who arose in times of crisis, but their rule was inherently temporary; no judge ever successfully transmitted his or her authority to a successor. This system protected the Israelites from their enemies, but it was inherently unstable and seems to be breaking down at the end of the book of Judges. Thus it is that in the days of the prophet Samuel, the Israelites turn to another, more permanent kind of political rule, deciding to establish a kingship, a dynastic form of rule that would transmit power from father to son. They did so, according to the Bible, not simply to stabilize their political life, but also because they saw how other peoples lived, and they wanted to be like them: "Give us a king," the people demand of the prophet Samuel, "to govern us like other nations" (1 Samuel 8:5). Israel's reason for establishing a king in the first place, in other words, was its desire to become like others, to imitate their leaders.

That wish is finally realized through Solomon, who not only secures the respect of other kings but literally becomes one of them. 1 Kings makes much of his relationship with other kings—his marriage to the daughter of the Egyptian king (1 Kings 3:1–2); his alliance with the Phoenician king Hiram (1 Kings 5); his visit with the Queen of Sheba (1 Kings 10)—and Solomon seems to get along with these and other rulers so well precisely because he is, or becomes, one of them, sharing their interests and values, even becoming a family member as in the case of Egypt. It is true that Solomon is greater than these other rulers—wiser, wealthier, more glorious—but the difference seems to be a matter of degree more than kind, Solomon developing a close kinship with the kings of other nations both literally and metaphorically.

For the biblical author, however, becoming like other peoples was not a positive development. Israel was supposed to be, in the words of the Torah, "a people that dwells apart," a unique and distinctive community defined in large part by its differences from other nations. Any attempt to become like other peoples was a threat to that distinctiveness, and this included the institution of the king, which nearly destroyed the Israelites' special relationship to God by leading the people into the worship of foreign gods. From this perspective, the account in 1 Kings is very different from the résumé of accomplishments ascribed to Azitiwada. On the surface, it too is a glorification of royal accomplishment, dwelling on how Solomon impressed all the rulers of the earth, but the judgment of foreign rulers is not the basis on which this narrative's author forms his own evaluation of Solomon; to the contrary, the approval of foreign kings signals that something is wrong, that Solomon is blurring the boundary that separates Israel from the nations. The more he accomplishes as king and the more he is admired by other kings, the more he comes to resemble them, and that, for the biblical author, is a trajectory that leads to disaster.

By way of an example, let us look more carefully at Solomon's relationship with the king of Egypt. In 1 Kings 3:1–2, the narrative reports that Solomon married the daughter of Pharaoh and brought her into the city of David while he built a palace for her. The marriage is mentioned in passing, without condemnation, and it is far from clear that the biblical author thought ill of it; the Torah itself allows for the possibility of intermarriage with the Egyptians or at least with Egyptian women, never explicitly forbidding such relationships and allowing the descendants of such relationships to fully join the community (Deuteronomy 23:8). But this is to describe the Bible's attitude toward individual Egyptians willing to join the Israelite community. Egypt itself was a different story, a symbol of oppressiveness and idolatry. It had enslaved Israel once before, nearly exterminating it, and a renewed relationship with it was dangerous, as Moses himself warns in the Torah: "You may indeed set over you a king whom the Lord your God will choose . . . even so, he must not acquire many horses for himself, or return the people to Egypt in order to acquire more horses, since the Lord has said to you, 'You must never return that way again'" (Deuteronomy 17:15–16). Biblical scholars think this passage, part of the larger Deuteronomistic history of which 1 Kings is part, actually has Solomon in mind because its description of the future king of Israel so precisely anticipates what Solomon does when he establishes a horse trade with Egypt. What disturbs Moses in this passage is his fear that a future king of Israel will undo everything he has achieved by reestablishing a relationship with Egypt, and that is what Solomon does by establishing commercial ties with Egypt—an act that the Bible interprets as a reversal of the Exodus.

Even worse than that, though, is the narrative's implication that by the end of his reign, Solomon has not merely allied himself with Egypt but has become a pharaoh himself. To complete all his building projects, we learn in 1 Kings 5 that Solomon had to impose forced labor not just on the Canaanites but on the Israelites themselves. The term "forced labor" recalls Israel's experiences as slaves in Egypt when it was forced by Pharaoh to advance his building projects, and it is the first of several parallels between Solomon and Pharaoh. Later, for example, we learn that Solomon faced opposition from a number of dissidents—Hadad the Edomite, Rezin the king of Damascus, and Jeroboam of the tribe of Ephraim—and Hadad and Jeroboam at least share certain characteristics with Moses. Hadad flees to Egypt and is accepted into the house of the Egyptian king just as Moses is adopted into the family of the Pharaoh, and later he leads a small-scale exodus back to his homeland (for those who know the Exodus story, Hadad's petition to Pharaoh has a familiar ring to it—"let me go"). Jeroboam flees to Egypt to escape being killed by Solomon just as Moses fled from Egypt to escape Pharaoh, and from there, after Solomon's death, he returns to liberate the Israelites from the hard labor imposed on them by the king (the parallel is even more pronounced in the Septuagint, which adds material not in the Masoretic text that makes Jeroboam even more Moses-like). If the narrative is casting Solomon's opponents as Moses, it follows that he himself has become the Pharaoh of the story.

Historically, in fact, the real-life Solomon conceivably could have modeled himself on the Egyptian king. Prior to the appearance of the Israelites in the twelfth century B.C.E., the land of Canaan was under Egyptian control; its rulers imbibed the political culture of their Egyptian lords, and Egypt continued to try to assert its influence well into the period of the monarchy, reinvading Canaan just a few years after Solomon's reign, according to the Bible. It is therefore well within the realm of historical possibility that an early Israelite king like Solomon actually patterned himself on the king of Egypt, as scholars have tried to show by noting parallels between the organization of Solomon's kingdom and the administrative structure of Egypt—the division of each into twelve districts, for example.

For ancient Israelites, however, the memory of Egyptian rule was colored by the story of the Exodus, in which the Pharaoh emerges as the arch-villain, and in this context the parallel between Solomon and Pharaoh takes on a very specific significance, casting Solomon in the worst possible light. Solomon's reign was supposed to be the culmination of the Exodus. The Israelites had reached Canaan many generations earlier, but it was only now, thanks to Solomon's success in securing the borders of Israel and building a house for God, that it can feel fully settled in the land, fully at home in the Promised Land. By aligning himself with Egypt, however—marrying the daughter of a pharaoh, trading in Egyptian horses, behaving like a pharaoh himself—Solomon not only spoils the redemptive ending of the Exodus story, he reverses it, forcing his people to relive its bondage in Egypt

Solomon's political success proved that there were many advantages to having a king—Israel was never wealthier or safer from its enemies than they were during Solomon's reign—but his pharaohlike qualities also reveal one of the flaws that was inherent in the institution of the kingship from its inception according to 1 Samuel. Israel's desire for such a ruler was a parroting of foreign ways, an act of assimilation, looking to other nations as a model when Israel should have been doing all it could to remain distinct from them. It is through Solomon that Israel realizes this desire for a king like other kings but it is also through him that this desire backfires; he replicates and even outdoes the accomplishments of other rulers, but he also comes to mirror their worst qualities—the arrogance, the exploitiveness, and the hard-heartedness.

This at least is how 1 Kings depicts the reign of Solomon. For those who prefer to think of Solomon as the ideal ruler, there is always the version of his life presented in 1–2 Chronicles, which eliminates almost all of Solomon's negative qualities, or at least mitigates them. There, for example, the king still marries the daughter of Pharaoh, but their relationship is downplayed; the Chronicler deletes almost all of the references to this marriage, and the one exception, 2 Chronicles 8:11, reflects an effort to make Solomon look more pious (1 Kings notes that Solomon built a palace for the daughter of Pharaoh; the Chronicler repeats this detail but adds that he did so not to honor her but to honor God by moving her out of Jerusalem lest her presence defile the sanctity of the ark). It is the cleaned-up account of Chronicles, written to minimize the problematic aspects of Solomon's life, that marks the beginning of his transformation into the ideal king that other rulers should emulate.

But if Chronicles had never been written, if all that the monarchs of Christendom and Islam had to work with for their knowledge of Solomon was Samuel and Kings, one wonders if he would have been so widely emulated. For not only does this version of Solomon prove unworthy of emulation, it calls the act of emulation itself into question, at least the emulation of one king by another. Would so many rulers have boasted of Solomonic judgment, would they have invested so much in replicating his Temple or his throne, if they and their subjects had understood what Solomon's political legacy really is: a lesson to the world that all human leaders are poor imitations of divine rule, including the wisest and most powerful among them?

7

Building Heaven on Earth

SOLOMON'S CONSTRUCTION OF THE TEMPLE, narrated in
1 Kings 5–8, marked a major turning point in the history not
just of his own people but of the world. As Solomon explains at
the time of its dedication, the Temple's most important function was to serve as a point of connection between Israel and
God. Before the Temple, God revealed himself to Israel, but
only rarely and in an intermittent way. In periods when it
lacked a prophet like Moses to intercede for them, Israel had
no way to establish contact with God, to seek divine assistance
in cases of emergency or to allay his anger. The Temple established a steady line of communication between God and Israel.
Whenever it sinned, Israel would be able to direct its prayers
toward the Temple and have confidence that God would take
notice. The monotheistic world would eventually learn to live
without temples, sacrifices, and priesthoods, which had become obsolete by the end of antiquity, but even now the Jerusalem Temple remains a model for how to worship God.

And not just for Jews. Muslim chroniclers report that after the early caliph Umar conquered Jerusalem and was shown the site of the Temple, he was moved to build a mosque nearby, the Al-Aksa mosque—one of the holiest sites of Islam—as a continuation of its cult. The Dome of the Rock was so closely associated with the Temple, in fact, that when medieval crusaders and pilgrims first saw it, they mistook it for the Temple itself. Islam's holiest site is the Kaaba, a cube-shaped, veil-covered shrine in Mecca, and it too seems modeled on the Temple, though Muslims believe that it is actually the Temple that is modeled on it, tracing the construction of the Kaaba beyond Solomon and back to Abraham.

Christians too look to the Temple as a model of sacred space. Of course, they have no need for the Temple itself, transferring its atoning properties to Christ, but many elements of especially Orthodox and Catholic worship are modeled on the Temple—the altars, the tables for sacred bread, and the screens that keep the sacred area hidden from the community—and show that it remains a paradigm of how to worship God. Like Islam, Christianity also produced its share of imitation Temples—the Church of the Holy Sepulchre in Jerusalem, where pilgrims could see Solomon's ring with their own eyes; the Hagia Sophia in present-day Istanbul, once the largest church in the world; and the old basilica of Saint Peter in Rome, with its twisted white marble columns that supposedly came from Solomon's Temple, among many other sacred spaces. Solomon not only transformed the worship of his own people; he set a precedent for how to make God manifest on earth, and nearly half the world's population would imitate this model.

Since the Temple was one of Solomon's most enduring achievements, it is worth our while to ask what made it such an extraordinary accomplishment. In a society as resource-poor as ancient Israel was, it was no mean achievement to build any kind of public building. Solomon's wealth and his alliance with

Phoenicia helped him to overcome the limits of Israelite architecture—he was able to secure high-quality timber and expert craftsmen from his friend Hiram of Tyre. We know from archaeology that the Phoenicians built impressive shrines for their own gods, but the challenge of building a house for God would have been daunting even for a builder with all the resources in the world, for its intended occupant resisted being confined to a single space, too restless, too elusive, or perhaps simply too overwhelmingly immense to be contained within a humanly constructed edifice. David had wanted to build a temple, preparing the way by erecting an altar in Jerusalem, but had ultimately failed to do so, and even Solomon wondered if such a building was possible. "Will God indeed dwell on earth?" he asks aloud. "Even heaven and highest heaven cannot contain you, much less this house that I have built!"

And yet Solomon was able to finish such a building, a modest structure in comparison with the religious structures of later ages but one that somehow linked Israel to the heavens. There was something about the Temple that distinguished it from any other building, that allowed it to exist both in the visible, material realm of mortals and in the unseen, otherworldly realm of God, and it is this transcendent quality, the Temple's capacity to span the distance between heaven and earth, that we seek to understand.

To understand Solomon's accomplishment in building the Temple, however, we must look beyond the surface of the biblical text. 1 Kings and Chronicles are sufficiently vague in their descriptions of the Temple to support varying reconstructions of its architecture, but they provide a fair amount of information. We learn there that it was sixty cubits long, twenty cubits wide, and thirty cubits high—that is, about ninety feet long, thirty feet wide, and forty-five feet high—and it was divided into three sections: a front porch area, a main sanctuary, and the inner sanctum known as the Holy of Holies. We are informed of how the Temple was decorated—its walls and floor were lined with fine cedar carved with the images of gourds and flowers, doors were engraved with cherubs and palm trees, and the whole of the house was overlaid with pure gold. The details are certainly impressive, suggesting a luminescent, awe-inspiring structure, but they do not amount to an explanation for how the Temple worked as a point of connection between Israel and God. Was the Temple's beauty and intricate design a way of conveying God's presence inside? Was it supposed to draw God's attention in some way? The Bible simply does not explain Solomon's architectural choices, why he designed the Temple as he did, or how its architectural elements made it a fitting medium for divine-human interaction.

The Bible does suggest that the objects kept within the Temple were essential to its sanctity. 1 Kings keeps a very careful inventory of the Temple's contents, describing in detail the two bronze pillars that stand in its front porch area; the bronze basis known as the molten sea; the gilded cherubs that stand guard in the Temple's inner sanctuary; the ten bronze basins that line the southern and northern sides of the Temple, the golden altar, and the gold and bronze vessels used for the sacrifice. It is probably not a coincidence that all of these objects were made out of or were covered in precious metal; the sheen was probably meant to suggest the sheen of divine presence, the glow of divine being that the biblical authors associated with scorching fire and blinding light. Many of these objects survived the destruction of Solomon's Temple in 586 B.C.E., carried off as loot to Babylon but eventually returned to the Israelites by the Persian king Cyrus, and their preservation was what made it possible to restore the Temple; they seem to be the actual point of connection with God, fashioned by men but radiating God's presence.

The most important of these objects was the ark of the covenant. Constructed during the days of the Exodus, the ark, or *aron ha-kodesh* as it is known in Hebrew, was used as a container for the tablets of the covenant revealed to Moses at Mount Sinai, but its importance was not limited to its role as a receptacle for sacred texts. It was a holy object in its own right. Scholars believe that it originally served as a place where God himself resided or at least made himself manifest on earth, functioning as a divine footstool or perhaps as a divine chariot that God would use to ride into battle; in this sense, it was functionally similar to the divine statues and thrones that other peoples used to make their gods manifest. It was not a likeness of God—idols were strictly forbidden by biblical law—but it did betoken God's presence, which was why it was so dangerous to approach or look into; one could no more look at the ark and survive than one could see God's face and live. To this day, long after the destruction of the Temple, long after the original ark went missing, long after Jews have developed other symbols of worship in its place, they still direct the prayer offered in synagogue toward an object named for the ark, the chest or niche in which the Torah scrolls are kept, in the belief that the ark must be present, if only in the virtual form of a replica, to feel that God is in the building.

Solomon did not construct the ark; he was not even the one to bring it to Jerusalem—his father, David, gets the credit for that—but it was he who secured it within the Temple, and its entrance into the Holy of Holies was like putting a plug in a socket, activating the Temple with divine energy. As soon as the priests place the ark within the sanctuary, the room fills up with a cloud so thick that the priests cannot see what they are doing. 1 Kings understands it as the divine presence, the "glory of the Lord," as it refers to the cloud—not God himself but an extension of his being—and its appearance is the moment at which this building of stone is transformed into a transcendent house of God.

But what about the rest of the Temple, described in such detail by the Bible? Why did the Temple have the dimensions that it did? What was the purpose of the other objects kept within it? Kings offers no answers to these questions, but Chronicles does; it suggests that the entire structure—not just the plan of the building itself but its contents and priestly service—were dictated by a blueprint or model that Solomon received from David, who received it in turn from God (1 Chronicles 28:11–19). Whereas Kings suggests that Phoenician artisans were responsible for the Temple's design, especially a half-Israelite, half-Tyrian craftsman named Hiram who designed the bronze furnishings in the Temple, Chronicles suggests that it was God himself who designed the Temple.

And why did God design it as he did? From Chronicles's brief reference arose the idea that this divinely revealed blueprint was the same plan that God used to design his heavenly abode—the heavens or the cosmos understood as a heavenly Temple. What linked the Temple to God in this reading of the Bible was not some physical object like the ark but a relationship of analogy or correspondence; the Temple was a kind of translation of the celestial Temple, rendering it in an earthly, material form that could be seen and comprehended by humans. What made it difficult to recognize this relationship was that the Bible's description of the Temple was incomplete and cryptic—it provided some hints about the Temple's architecture but not enough to understand how the Temple's design corresponded to the design of the universe. To discern that, one needed an ability to see beyond the surface of things, the kind of extraordinary knowledge that Solomon possessed, a knowledge of the hidden aspects of existence. In antiquity and the Middle Ages, interpreters used magic and mystical techniques to recover such knowledge, composing texts that purported to reveal the architecture of the heavenly Temple. In more recent times biblical interpreters began to rely on what we would now call science to understand the correspondence— physics, geometry, astronomy, and other methods by which one can look beyond the visible world to discern its hidden architecture.

And we are talking not about scientific crackpots but about some of the most brilliant minds of the day—who else, after all, would possess the kind of intellectual ability required to understand the wisdom encoded into Solomon's Temple? This effort to understand the encrypted architecture of the Temple produced some stunning works of erudition in the sixteenth and seventeenth centuries in particular, an age that saw no contradiction between the Bible and science and that used each to illumine the other. At the end of the sixteenth century, for example, two Spanish Jesuits, Hieronymo Prado and Juan Bautista Villalpando, undertook an ambitious commentary on the Temple that enlisted cutting-edge architectural and mathematical knowledge to explain the design of the Temple as described in Ezekiel 40–48, which they assumed had the same basic design as Solomon's Temple. Prado died before the final two volumes were complete but Villalpando went on to complete the project, going so far as to develop new mathematical instrumentation to explicate what he imagined as an exquisitely complex architectural design that mirrored the structure of the human body and the cosmos. The reconstruction of the Temple that resulted from this effort had a major impact on early modern architecture, guiding the construction of great European edifices like the monastery at El Escorial in Spain as well as Spanish churches built in the New World. Another scientist who sought to understand the Temple's encrypted architecture was none other than Sir Isaac Newton, who tried to improve on Villalpando's effort by consulting neglected Jewish sources like the Talmud and, by doing better math, writing a dissertation in which he undertook to more accurately calculate the Temple's measurements. The tradition culminated at the end of the century with the construction of three-dimensional models of the Temple. The most famous was constructed in Amsterdam by a rabbi, Jacob Judah Leon (subsequently known as Leon Templo because of his association with the Temple), and it attracted the interest of some of Europe's leading architects and intellectuals, including, judging from a copy of a book by Leon Templo found in his library, Spinoza.

The perception of the Temple as a reflection of the hidden design of the cosmos lives on into our day, preserved by the secret organization known as the Freemasons. Historians tell us that Freemasonry developed in the seventeenth and eighteenth centuries, perhaps as an offshoot of the secret society of mystics known as the Rosecrucians and reflecting the influence of early modern scientists like Francis Bacon and Isaac Newton and their ideas about King Solomon and his Temple. In their own mythology, however, the Freemasons are the heirs to the chief architect of the Temple, Hiram Abiff—not the king but Hiram the craftsman, who fashions the bronze objects kept in the Temple (Hiram Abiff reflects the spelling of his name in 2 Chronicles, Huram-Abi). What distinguishes a Freemason like Hiram from an ordinary artisan or construction worker is his possession of esoteric knowledge that includes not just secret passwords and initiation rites but geometry and other arcane scientific knowledge that can reveal the secrets of the universe. This knowledge is what gets Hiram killed, according to Masonic myth: he was murdered by three other masons when he refused to reveal his secrets to them. The Freemasons believe themselves to be the heirs to these secrets, which they too use to construct a kind of mystical architecture—buildings that encode a hidden, cosmic design (some believe that all the monuments in Washington, D.C., including the Washington Monument, are the work of Masonic architects, a debatable interpretation to say the least, but for a clear-cut example you can tour the Masonic Temple, located in Washington on the corner of 16th Street NW and S Street NW).

Freemasonry seems to be alive and well to this day, but

Masonic belief regarding the Temple is a vestige of ideas that no longer resonate for many of the rest of us, reflecting an early modern view of architecture that envisioned God himself as the "High Architect of the World" (in the words of Henry Wotton's *Elements of Architecture*, published in 1624) and human architects as his imitators. Early modern architects saw the Temple as the prototype of this kind of architecture, fusing a mystical yearning to understand God with the scientific/mathematical quest to penetrate the secrets of the universe, but as even some early modern architects themselves recognized, their efforts to understand the Temple read far more into the biblical text than was really there. Such was the argument, for example, of one of the most brilliant architects of this period, Christopher Wren, who worked at a time when the Bishop of London was insisting that all the churches of his city imitate the magnificent Temple of Solomon. Wren admired the Temple, but he did not see the hidden perfection that others like Villalpando did, accusing him of simply inventing some of the architectural features that he attributed to the Temple.

Three centuries after Wren we know much more about architecture in Solomon's day thanks to archaeological revelations about temple-building in the age of Solomon's Temple. As we have noted, there is no archaeological evidence of the Temple itself, but scholars have excavated other temples in the region, both in Canaan itself and in neighboring regions like Lebanon and Syria, including one at a site called Ain Dara, which existed in the same century that Solomon built his temple, and these temples are very similar in their design to the Temple as it is described by Kings. It turns out that many of the elements ascribed to the Temple in 1 Kings—the tripartite design, the two pillars that stood at the entrance to the Temple, the cherubs that guarded the ark of the covenant—have counterparts in other temples, especially those found just to the north of Israel, suggesting that it was no divine plan or heavenly

model that guided the Temple's construction but an earlier ancient Near Eastern tradition of how to build a divine abode.

The discovery that Solomon's Temple reflects local architectural tradition sheds some light on the symbolism and design of Solomon's Temple, but what it also does is undercut our
impression of it as an exceptional structure. Historically speaking, it was not the unique, supernatural construction that Jews
have long believed it to be but a conventional building, hardly
distinguishable from other temples in the neighborhood except
perhaps for its avoidance of divine images, and even that difference may not be as great as it seems (some scholars note that
other peoples in the environs of ancient Israel, including some
Phoenicians, also avoided visualizing their gods in anthropo-
morphic form—it is possible that even the Temple's aniconism
is a conventional trait). It was still an accomplishment for Solomon to build such a temple, if he did build it, but the accomplishment was a relative one. It signaled Solomon's success in
consolidating his kingdom and developing a profitable economic relationship with Phoenicia, and its construction, along
with the palace that Solomon built for himself, raised Jerusalem
to the level of other royal capitals in the region—all impressive
feats for a young king of a young kingdom—but it was nothing
compared with the great temples of Egypt and Babylon.

Or the great temples of our age, for that matter. We now
know nearly as much as Solomon did about how to build a
house for God, perhaps more than he did. Posterity's attempts
to imitate it—the Hagia Sophia, the Dome of the Rock, the El
Escorial—not only rival Solomon's accomplishment, they often
outdo it in scale, expense, complexity, and aesthetic appeal. In
2010, the controversial Brazilian religious leader Edir Macado
has announced plans to build yet another replica of the Temple
that will cost $200 million, stand eighteen stories high, and seat
ten thousand people. It will dwarf the building that it seeks to
replicate. But even with all our vaulting architectural ambi-

tion—and our technical ability to realize that ambition in a way that Solomon never could have imagined—there is still something elusive about the original Temple, something incomprehensible about its capacity to encompass the immensity of divine presence *despite* its small size, or to propel the voice of prayer into heaven *despite* the inert weight of its stones. The Temple's imitators inspire awe and reverence; they dazzle, inspire, and leave one feeling very small and humble, but if one knows enough about the arts of design and engineering, their mystery will reveal itself. Not so with Solomon's Temple. However carefully one scrutinizes the biblical text, however close the resemblance to other ancient temples, there is still something elusive about it, a quality that geometry cannot decipher or archaeology retrieve because it may not be an architectural effect at all but something invisible, immaterial, dimensionless, a quality beyond the reach of those without divine wisdom.

Whatever it was that made the Temple such a special building, we can say this: the act of building it changed everything for the Israelites, and for Solomon in particular. According to the Bible, as we have noted, its construction was an important turning point in Israel's history. It may have been more than that, the narrative signaling that it was perhaps *the* central turning point of biblical history, both a climactic moment of one formative experience and the beginning of another. According to a medieval Jewish chronicle known as *Seder Olam Zuta*, Solomon's Temple stood for 410 years, a number that is suspiciously close to the 480 years that separate the Temple from the Exodus, and the math tempts one to suggest that its construction was the actual chronological midpoint of biblical history. Whether that is the case or not, the Bible does depict the Temple's construction as the symbolic midpoint of Israel's history. On the one hand, it marks a happy ending to the Exodus, a long saga that is now finally over: Israel is able to settle down as signified by the construction of a permanent resting place for God. On the other hand, the building of the Temple is also the beginning of the opposite kind of story, the tragic narrative that unfolds over the rest of Kings and that will culminate with the Israelites forced back into a life of homelessness and subjugation during the Babylonian exile. The Temple is smack in the middle between Exodus and Exile, hope and despair—always and forever the twin story lines of Jewish life—and its construction is precisely that moment when the two experiences converge on one other, the realization of redemption and the beginning of its undoing at the same time.

The building of the Temple has exactly this double significance within the life of Solomon as well. Everything that happens up until this moment has been anticipated in advance. God promised Solomon that he would become greater, wealthier, and more honored than any other king. That has happened. Even earlier, God had promised through the prophet Nathan that Solomon would build the Temple. That has happened now too. But God never gives us a clear glimpse of what is supposed to follow once these things have been achieved. The final chapters of Solomon's life are unplanned for in a way that isn't true for the events in 1 Kings 1–8; he begins to deviate from the plan prescribed by his name, to act from his own impulses rather than from the desires of God or his father, David, to make decisions that derail the way biblical history was supposed to unfold. We do not know exactly why this change occurs but we do get some sense of when it begins to manifest itself, and it is the building of the Temple that marks the difference between the two stages of Solomon's life as if here, too, God had planned out the story only through to the middle, not foreseeing what would happen afterward, or somehow losing control from that point.

I cannot explain what it is about the Temple that makes its construction such an important turning point in the life of Sol-

omon and his people, but I do know that I am not the only interpreter to see it in this way. Both early Jewish and Christian
interpreters recognized the period after the Temple's construction as one of newfound independence for Solomon. It was in
this period, more specifically, that the king formed his alliance
with Asmodeus and other demons, an ungodly source of insight and power that allowed the king to transgress boundaries
imposed on him by the Lord—ironically, in fact, it was the
Temple itself that precipitated this alliance, for Solomon found
that the only way he could surmount the challenge of building
it was to turn to the demons for help (variants of this tradition
are found both in the Talmud, in tractate *Gittin* 68a, and in the
Christian *Testament of Solomon*, purportedly the final reflections
of the king but really a pseudepigraphic composition written
sometime in late antiquity). Somewhere in the background of
this legend lies a recognition of the Temple's construction as a
breaking point in the narrative, the moment when Solomon
begins to act independent of what God had in mind for him.

In Kings' account of what happens next, Solomon's in-
creasing independence from God leads to tragic consequences,
the king eventually breaking from God altogether to follow
after other gods. But precisely because, once he builds the
Temple, Solomon no longer has a predetermined destiny, we
should not, even having looked ahead to the end of the story in
1 Kings 11, be too quick to assume that we know how things
will turn out. Solomon's descent into sin is a surprise, something we could not have anticipated from Nathan's prophecy in
2 Samuel 7 or the prediction encrypted into the letters of Solomon's name, but according to some interpreters there is yet
another surprise beyond it, a final act of self-transformation in
which the king repairs his relationship with God. Now, neither
Kings nor Chronicles ever mentions such an incident, but less
authoritative accounts do, and they will be our guide for much
of the rest of the book, not because they tell us what actually

happened to the king but because, by recounting the story of Solomon's final years in ways that differ from the tragic ending of Kings, they make the king's life truly open-ended, much as we'd like to believe our own lives to be.

One of the reasons that Solomon is so honored by Jews, Christians, and Muslims is that, by building the Temple, he made it possible for the sinful to change the destiny decreed for them by God. God might have erased the sinner's name from the book of life, dooming him or her, but by performing the Temple rites, offering the requisite sacrifices on the Day of Atonement, one could change that fate and have one's name written back in. This may be the true secret of the Temple's power—not some magical object hidden within its interior or some strange symbolism encrypted into its design but simply the way it opened up for people, invisibly and inexplicably, new possibilities for redemption. In other words, what made the Temple such an important turning point, what made Israel's history after its construction feel so unpredictable, capricious, and yet still not without hope, is the power it bestowed on its worshipers to rewrite the end of their own stories even when that ending had already been decreed by God. Given his role in building the Temple, given his role in opening up for others the possibility of revising their destiny, it seems only fair that we grant Solomon such a possibility himself, and that will be one of our goals in this book's final chapter—to allow him a chance to rewrite the end of his life.

Before then, however, there are a few other questions that we need to address about Solomon, the first of which is particularly relevant at this moment in history. As I write this, the world is struggling to recover from the worst financial crisis since the Great Depression. At such a time, Solomon becomes all the more interesting for his astonishing ability to generate wealth. The fortune that Solomon acquired over the course of his reign is staggering even by today's standards: the weight of the gold that came to him in just a single year amounted to 660 talents, twenty-five tons, not to mention the silver, the precious stones, the costly spices, the fine wood, the garments, the exotic animals, and the ivory that he was able to import. Who better to seek financial wisdom from than Solomon, who excelled all the kings of the earth not just in his wisdom but in his wealth?

Judging from a quick check of a local bookstore, in fact, where one can find volumes with titles like *The Richest Man in the World: King Solomon's Secrets to Success, Wealth and Happiness;* and *Succeed Thru Need: The Power of Solomonics,* many still look to the king for this kind of wisdom. Such tracts can be exploitative and manipulative, cheap rip-offs of the book of Proverbs, and I doubt anyone will become rich by reading them, but they pose a question that has long fascinated readers about the king's story, including some very important readers whose efforts to find the source of Solomon's wealth have shaped the fortunes of hundreds of millions of people, and it is the question we will try to address in the next chapter: how did Solomon become so rich?

8

———◆◌◆———

Mining for Solomon's Gold

NEITHER KINGS NOR CHRONICLES ever explains how Solomon manages to become so prosperous, but that has not stopped people from trying to discover the source of his wealth. In fact, the assumption that the source of Solomon's wealth was still findable—that if one knew what he knew, one could become as wealthy as he was—inspired one of the greatest treasure hunts in history, the search for the source of Solomon's gold. H. Rider Haggard's *King Solomon's Mines,* one of the most popular adventure novels of the nineteenth century and the inspiration for a dozen or more Hollywood movies including the Indiana Jones series, is a fictional account of such a quest, an attempt to find the source of Solomon's wealth in Africa, but it has real life antecedents that go back to at least the fifteenth century, traversing every continent of the world with the possible exception of Antarctica, and that continue into our own day. This chapter tells the story of that larger quest, not to find Solo-

mon's treasure, which like so much else about the king is beyond our reach, but to see if the search for it yields any insights
into his life story.

The problem that faced those seeking the source of Solomon's wealth was both an interpretive one and a geographical
one: where to look. Solomon's wealth seemed to be based on an
accumulation of gold, silver, ivory, and other precious commodities, most of which cannot be found within the land of Canaan. That implies that he imported these commodities from
somewhere else, but from where, and in exchange for what, are
not made clear. But interpreters did notice certain clues in the
biblical text which pointed them in a specific direction—two
names, Ophir and Tarshish, mentioned in 1 Kings 9–10:

> King Solomon built a fleet of ships at Ezion-geber, which is
> near Elath on the shore of the Red Sea, in the land of Edom.
> Hiram sent his servants with the fleet, sailors who knew the
> sea, with the servants of Solomon. They went to Ophir, and
> took from there four hundred and twenty talents of gold,
> which they brought to King Solomon. [1 Kings 9:26–28]

> The king had a fleet of ships of Tarshish at sea with the fleet
> of Hiram. Once every three years, the fleet of ships of Tar-
> shish would arrive laden with gold, silver, ivory, apes, and
> peacocks. [1 Kings 10:22]

The actual meaning of Ophir and Tarshish in these passages is
a bit ambiguous. Ophir, a word that came to be associated with
fine gold, seems to be a specific place, but possibly a mythical
one like El Dorado, while the "ships of Tarshish" probably did
not mean ships headed for a specific location but rather a specific kind of vessel, a ship built to go across the ocean. Whatever their real meaning, these words came to be understood as
specific geographical locations, and that meant in turn that Solomon's gold was potentially retrievable. Figure out where Ophir

and Tarshish were located, certain enterprising interpreters believed, then figure out a way to get there, and one could rediscover the source of his wealth and perhaps even become as wealthy as he was.

In recent years, the perceived remoteness and inaccessibility of Ophir and Tarshish have recommended them as extraterrestrial names (on Mars, there are several places named for Ophir, like the Ophir Chasma, a huge Martian canyon, while "Tarshish" was recently under consideration by Israel's Hebrew Language Academy as a possible name for Neptune). For most of the past two thousand years, in fact, Ophir and Tarshish were thought beyond reach; all commentators could do was speculate about their location without ever hoping to reach these places themselves. That situation changed at the end of the fifteenth century, however, when improved cartography and better ship construction meant that ships could now travel much farther than had previously been possible. All these advances were thought to have been known already to the all-knowing Solomon, but his wisdom had been lost. As Spanish, Portuguese, and English ships ventured into the world, explorers saw themselves as rediscovering this knowledge, convinced that it would lead them, among other places, to the source of Solomon's gold.

Here is what the would-be discoverers of Solomon's wealth knew, or thought they knew, about the location of Ophir and Tarshish, working with the few clues that the Bible provides:

1) Ophir and Tarshish were far away. 1 Kings 10:22 seems to suggest that it took Solomon's ships a total of three years to complete a round-trip journey—a year and a half to get there and the same amount of time to return. What the verse actually says is merely that the ships of Tarshish would arrive every three years, which does not necessarily mean that the trip took three years, but that is what it was understood to mean.

2) To reach these places, Solomon's ships had to travel
   east, not traversing the Mediterranean but leaving the
   Red Sea port of Ezion-Geber and presumably travel-
   ing from there down into the Gulf of Aden and the
   Arabian Sea. The cargo that these ships brought back
   included ivory and monkeys, which suggested that
   Ophir and Tarshish were somewhere in Africa or Asia.
3) References elsewhere in the Bible—in particular Isaiah
   60:9—suggested that these places were islands: "the islands wait for me, the ships of Tarshish . . ."

On the basis of such evidence, European seafarers settled on
what it was that they were looking for—a port or islands somewhere in Africa, India, or the Far East, but before they could get
there, a very serious practical obstacle remained. It seemed to
take a year and a half for Solomon's ships to reach these places.
That was far too long to travel, and besides: between here and
there stood hostile Muslims who, if they knew where Solomon's
gold was located, were not about to share it with Christians.

The sailor who figured out a way around these problems is
far better known for other discoveries—he was none other than
Christopher Columbus himself—but his exegetical ingenuity
should not be overlooked. We know from Columbus's writings
that he studied the Bible and other ancient sources like Josephus for clues about the location of Ophir and Tarshish, which
he assumed were the same place, and from such sources he surmised that Ophir was an island located in India or China, perhaps even the same island that Marco Polo had learned of during his journey to China, the island once called Cipango and
what we now know as Japan. In contrast to Marco Polo, however—and this was one of Columbus's great exegetical insights—he realized he did not need to travel east to find it
since, by his day, it was known that the world was round; indeed, he believed it would take him much less time to reach
Ophir and Tarshish if he traveled west—just a few weeks rather

than the year and a half that it had taken Solomon's fleet. Not only did such a route seem quicker, it was also safer, since it would bypass Muslim-controlled seas.

Columbus's journey ended up taking a little longer than he thought—he greatly underestimated the size of the earth—but he eventually found what he was looking for on the island of Hispaniola, where Haiti and the Dominican Republic are now located. There, he spent a decade searching for gold, and when it became clear that he had been mistaken, he was sent back to Spain. In Columbus's mind, however, the problem was not that he had been wrong to look for Ophir but that he had been looking in the wrong place. Further study led him to modify his views about its whereabouts, and in 1502 the Spanish monarchs gave him another chance. Landing on the shores of Central America, between what is now Honduras and Panama, he came across a native who, when asked by a translator where they were, seemed to respond, "Ophir." Soon thereafter, Columbus dispatched a letter to Ferdinand and Isabella to place Solomon's gold at their disposal.

Whether Columbus had actually found Ophir and Tarshish was much debated by contemporary scholars. Some were convinced that he had, including Thomas Bozio, a sixteenth century Christian scholar, who thought that Columbus was fulfilling God's intentions for the world by finding Ophir and Tarshish and who in fact found in the Bible (in its Latin translation) what he took to be a prophecy of Columbus's discovery: "Who are these that fly like a cloud, and like doves [Latin: *columbae*] to their windows? For the coastlands shall wait for me, the ships of Tarshish first, to bring your children from far away, their silver and gold with them" (Isaiah 60:8–9). Not everyone was persuaded that Columbus had been looking in the right place, however. Throughout the sixteenth century, a debate raged about whether Ophir was to be found in the Americas. The arguments against a location in the Americas were formidable—why didn't Solomon's ships bring llamas back with them if they were coming back from South America? How did they get across the sea without a compass? But even those who rejected Columbus's views did not draw the conclusion that the whole search was in vain—they simply started looking for Ophir and Tarshish elsewhere, moving from South America to the South Pacific and Africa. It was during this period, for example, that a Spanish expedition led by Álvaro de Mendaña, a nephew of the Peruvian viceroy, discovered what they took to be the source of Solomon's gold on a chain of islands not far from what is now New Guinea—islands consequently known as the Solomon Islands.

While the Spanish took the lead in the search for Solomon's gold (ironically, today's biblical scholars suspect that Tarshish was actually in Spain itself), their domination of the seas was sharply contested by the Portuguese and English, who soon joined in the search themselves. It was the Portuguese who extended Europe's search into Africa, a location suggested by the inclusion of ivory among the treasures brought back from Ophir (it also did not escape the notice of explorers that the name *Africa* itself bore a certain resemblance to Ophir). In 1502, for example, a Portuguese sailor named Thomas Lopez, arriving at a trading port in eastern Africa known as Sofala, was greeted by Muslims who claimed to have discovered certain native texts that reported Solomon's ships removing gold from a nearby site once every three years—this according to a Renaissance map publisher named Abraham Ortelius, and the identification of Sofala with Ophir was buttressed by the Septuagint, where the name Ophir is preceded by an initial *S*, *Sophir*. It is not an accident that H. Rider Haggard's *King's Solomon's Mines* imagines its English adventurers following a course to Solomon's treasure in Africa laid out by an earlier Portuguese explorer, the ill-fated Jose Silvestra. In real life, Portuguese explorers sought Solomon's gold in Africa well into the nineteenth century, before the British forced them to leave to make way for their own fortune-seeking.

The English had joined the quest for Solomon's gold long before, thanks to the theft of a Spanish map. The Spanish and the Portuguese closely guarded the maps that recorded their navigational discoveries, but in 1527 an Englishman named Robert Thorne was able to smuggle a Spanish map out of Seville and he used it to publish the first English map of the world. Among the navigational secrets disclosed by this map was the alleged location of Tarshish and Ophir, placed southwest of China in what seems like the East Indies (they are labeled in Latin, "islands of Tarshish and Offir most wealthy").

No less reputable an explorer than Sir Walter Raleigh seemed to accept the information in Thorne's map, concluding

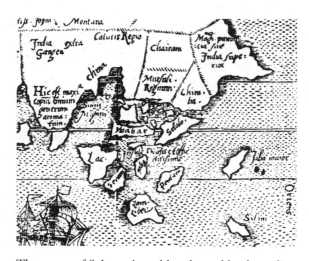

The source of Solomon's wealth as located by the earliest English map of the world. Ophir and Tarshish appear as part of a cluster of islands in the center of the picture corresponding to present-day Indonesia, marked by the words *Insule Tharsis et Offir ditissime* (the islands of Tarshish and Ophir most wealthy). (Reprinted with permission from the Bancroft Library, University of California, Berkeley)

that Ophir and Tarshish were near the Molucca Islands in Indonesia—and some actually looked in that region, including John Davis, the first Englishman to reach the Falkland Islands, who sought Ophir in Sumatra. Other English explorers looked elsewhere. In 1577, an English pirate named Martin Frobisher discovered what appeared to be a great trove of gold on an island in the Canadian Arctic Circle now known as Baffin Island. While much of the gold was later found to be worthless iron pyrite (fool's gold), some believed that Frobisher had discovered Ophir. The English search for Ophir expanded as the British Empire expanded, moving by the nineteenth century into Africa and even Australia. The most illustrious Englishman to look for Ophir probably was Sir Richard Burton, the nineteenth century scholar/adventurer known for his translation of the *Arabian Nights*, who searched for Ophir throughout Arabia, East Africa, and India.

In retrospect, all this searching seems like a kind of collective madness, calling to mind fictional characters like the conquistador Lope de Aguirre in Werner Herzog's film *Aguirre Wrath of God*, who loses his mind in a fruitless search through the Amazon for the gold of the legendary El Dorado (which, as it happens, was also identified as Ophir by the seventeenth century priest Ferdinand de Montesinos). At the time, however, those looking for Solomon's gold thought of themselves as engaged in an utterly rational quest. What had allowed Solomon to acquire all his wealth, after all, was knowledge that included an understanding of distant regions and how to reach them, and those looking for Solomon's gold saw themselves not just as treasure hunters but as seekers of this knowledge. As Columbus himself suggests in a letter to Ferdinand and Isabella, the motive was the desire to "know the secrets of the world," the secrets of far-off places.

Eventually, in fact, the search for Solomon's gold became a kind of scientific quest, drawing on archaeology, linguistics, and anthropology to help find what it was looking for. Some 370 years after Thomas Lopez arrived in the port of Sofala, in 1871 a German geologist named Karl Mauch returned to the region in search of Solomon's gold (Mauch's quest, so widely publicized that others were reporting from the site of his discovery before he even reached it himself, was one of the inspirations for Haggard's *King's Solomon's Mines*, though Haggard denied any influence). Following information gleaned from Portuguese sources, Mauch trekked into the hinterland of southern Africa to the Great Zimbabwe, the immense stone ruins of an ancient city. The idea that the site could have been constructed by indigenous Africans, as it really was, never occurred to Mauch. To his mind, the site bore traces of Solomonic influence—he recognized among the ruins a structure that seemed a copy of the Temple and another that he took to be the palace of the Queen of Sheba—leading him to the conclusion that what he had found was the capital of her fabled kingdom, as well as the source of Solomon's gold. After news of his discovery spread in Europe, it didn't take long for others to ransack the site.

What distinguishes Mauch's quest from the earlier efforts that we have been describing to find Solomon's gold is its effort to apply not just exegetical but scientific reasoning to the problem. Clever biblical interpretation was no longer sufficient to establish a Solomonic connection; one needed external corroboration, evidence independent of the Bible, and Mauch endeavored to find such evidence. One proof emerged from an improvised analysis of wood splinters found at the site: Mauch noticed that they resembled a cedar pencil he was using to take notes, and on that basis made a connection to the cedar of Lebanon used to build the Temple. Other evidence drew on comparative religion: natives whom he interviewed spoke of sacrifices that seemed to preserve elements of biblical ritual. And Mauch cited linguistic evidence as well—a supposed etymological link between the names Zimbabwe and Sheba. By the early twentieth century, scholars had debunked Mauch's interpretation, linking the site to the local Shona people, and in the interim his theory had done much damage to the site—and to sub-Saharan Africa more broadly—by drawing imperialist attention to it. As easy as it is to see the problems with his reasoning now, however, Mauch was trying to be scientific, and his expedition was a kind of intermediate stage between the religiously motivated treasure-hunting of Columbus and the modern archaeological excavation.

Another case from the same period involved the alleged discovery related to Solomon's ally and shipping partner, Hiram of Tyre. The decipherment of Phoenician in the eighteenth century had an immense impact on the study of ancient history, revealing an enterprising ancient Mediterranean civilization that was thought to have played a catalytic role in the development of Greek—and hence European—culture (as Haggard once put it, the Phoenicians were the English of the ancient world without the English honor). By the second half of the nineteenth century, volumes of Phoenician inscriptions had been published, and the ongoing excavation of Phoenician sites—the first biblical sites to undergo modern excavation—promised many new discoveries. All this had relevance for Solomon because of his close association with Hiram, his Phoenician partner in naval expeditions to Ophir and Tarshish. The Phoenicians, this new evidence established, were in fact a great seafaring people. Not only did they settle throughout North Africa and the Mediterranean reaching all the way to Spain, but, according to Herodotus, they had even managed to circumnavigate Africa. The idea that the Phoenicians had made it beyond the Mediterranean world thus seemed within the realm of the historically possible, and scholars could now use epigraphy, the study of inscriptions, to trace their far-reaching travels into southern Africa and beyond.

Mauch himself thought he discerned Phoenician influence on the ruins of the Great Zimbabwe, and some believed that they had made it all the way to the New World, for just three years after Mauch's discovery of the kingdom of Sheba in South Africa, a Phoenician inscription turned up in Brazil, on the Parahyba River. The inscription, allegedly left behind by the survivors of a Phoenician shipwreck, does not mention Solomon directly, but it includes details that suggest these sailors were from one of the ships dispatched for Ophir, mentioning that they were servants of Hiram and noting that their journey had begun at Ezion-Geber, the Red Sea port built by Solomon, according to 1 Kings. Earlier Christian scholars had suggested Solomon's gold came from South America—one popular theory connected it to Peru, citing as evidence a rare word used in 2 Chronicles 3:6 to describe the gold that Solomon used to build the Temple, *parvayim*, or *parouim* in its Greek translation, which to premodern etymologists seemed to resemble the word *Peru*. The discovery of the Parahyba inscription seemed to provide archaeological corroboration of this theory, the kind of evidence that was being used to illumine the Phoenician presence in the Mediterranean, and while it was soon recognized as a hoax, it was convincing enough to fool a highly respected twentieth century scholar of Semitics, Cyrus Gordon, who republished it in 1968 as an authentic inscription.

The quest for the source of Solomon's wealth has produced so many false leads over the centuries—and has done so much damage by legitimizing the looting of sites like the Great Zimbabwe—that one would expect scholars to have given up by now, but remarkably it continues into our own time, albeit in more scientifically sophisticated forms. The most recent attempt that I know about is an ongoing excavation in Jordan directed by Thomas Levy of the University of San Diego and the Jordanian archaeologist Mohammad Najjar. In 2008, in fact, Levy and Najjar announced the discovery of a massive copper mining operation at Khirbet en Nahas in southern Jordan, which they date to the tenth and ninth centuries B.C.E., the time of Solomon. More than seventy years ago, in the 1930s, another leading archaeologist, the famous rabbi-archaeologist Nelson Glueck, thought he had found traces of Solomon's mining operation in the Negev desert—not the source of his gold but the source of the copper that he used to trade for other kinds of wealth—but by the 1980s scholars had come to believe that he had misdated the evidence. Najjar and Levy (who was once assistant director of the Nelson Glueck School of Archaeology) are being careful not to repeat Glueck's mistakes; their dating of their discovery is based on the most rigorous scientific methodology possible—not just pottery analysis but radiocarbon dating—and they are careful to leave the question of who exactly built the site an open one since that is not a question that the evidence clearly resolves. Judging from their press releases, however, they evidently want the public to believe that this was a Solomonic mining operation or, in other words, that what they have discovered may well be the elusive source of the king's wealth.

It is certainly possible that Levy and Najjar have discovered what lies behind the biblical account of Solomon's wealth—a massive mining operation—but what we have seen here suggests that we should probably hesitate before drawing any final conclusions. Five hundred years of searching for the source of Solomon's wealth has uncovered a significant amount of what seems like corroborating evidence—etymological connections between biblical place names like Ophir and Sheba and known geographical sites; archaeological ruins in Israel, Africa, and elsewhere; and, of course, much treasure, but all of it has proven illusory (fool's gold, as it were), without a real connection to Solomon. Perhaps there is some historical core to the Bible's description of Solomon's wealth, but to find the source of that wealth one must, in effect, rewrite the biblical texts, adding details that make it possible to connect the vague information they provide about Ophir and Tarshish to the knowable world. There simply is no other way to find the source of Solomon's gold, even for the most sophisticated, scientifically objective archaeologist.

Consider, for example, the idea that Solomon's wealth comes from a mining operation. As Levy and Najjar acknowledge, the origin of this idea is a work of fiction. Haggard's novel *King Solomon's Mines*, which itself was drawing on a still earlier tradition that one can trace back at least as far as the Renaissance, when advocates of mining were looking for religious arguments to overcome objections to it as a form of impudent and overreaching curiosity. The Bible itself nowhere suggests that Solomon's wealth derived from mining, though exegetes uncovered a reference to it in the word *Cabul*, which appears in I Kings 9:13—the name of a territory given by Solomon to Hiram in exchange for his help in building the Temple—which they mistakenly derived from the mineral *cobalt* and took to mean that the region was a mining district. The idea of Solomon's Mines was probably inspired by biblical passages, like Job 28, which associate the search for wisdom with mining, and may also reflect the influence of the medieval legend of Alexander the Great, who, it was thought, sought to conquer not just the world but the secrets hidden beneath its surface. To connect the archaeology to the biblical evidence, then, Levy and Najjar have to rely on a detail not in any biblical text but invented by later readers who were looking for the same thing that they were.

But those searching for this wealth do more than read into the biblical text; they also miss what it does say. Like Solomon's wisdom, his wealth was meant to be an extraordinary attribute that distinguished the king from all other rulers: "I also give you what you have not asked," God tells him in his dream, "both riches and honor all your life; no other king shall compare with you." As if to prove this point, the other potentates featured in 1 Kings 1–11—Hiram and the Queen of Sheba— are also described as wealthy, but none can rival Solomon's fortune because his wealth was miraculous, something that others could achieve not through their own effort but only through an act of divine intervention.

This is also why, according to the Bible, Solomon's wealth is irretrievable. At several points it describes the king's possessions as unparalleled or unprecedented: the almug wood that he uses for his palace is unlike any wood that has ever been seen (1 Kings 10:12); and nothing like his ivory throne exists in any kingdom (10:12). This isn't empty hyperbole, but an attempt to underscore the irreproducibility of Solomon's wealth. So too is a story that appears at the very end of 1 Kings. One of Solomon's successors, Jehoshaphat, did try to make it back to Ophir, and he built a new fleet of ships at Ezion-Geber to travel for this purpose, but they were wrecked before they even left port. The ships were of the same quality; they were headed in the right direction, but they never make it because Jehoshaphat lacks the divine support that Solomon enjoyed.

What those searching for Solomon's wealth miss, in other words, is how their quest for this wealth runs against the grain of the biblical text. It isn't simply that 1 Kings fails to provide enough information or that its information is too vague; its author did not believe that Solomon's treasure was accessible to others, and his description is designed to underscore that fact, exciting the reader's admiration and cupidity through detailed description of how much treasure the king possessed but leaving it just beyond reach. Perhaps some day archaeology will find the location of Ophir, but if that ever happens, what they learn about the historical Solomon and where his wealth really came from will come at the expense of the biblical Solomon whose fortune is meant to be unfathomable.

From Riches to Rags

To be fair to those seeking Solomon's treasure, however, we shouldn't think of them all as greedy treasure hunters or reckless adventurers. Some were motivated by scholarly curiosity, seeking to illumine the secrets of the biblical text; others had pious motives, searching for Solomon's gold in the hope of doing God's work with it as Solomon himself had done with his wealth. There is evidence, for example, that Columbus's quest for Ophir was religiously motivated. In the very year he discovered America, his patrons Ferdinand and Isabella reclaimed Spain for Christianity, a feat that convinced Columbus they would reconquer Jerusalem and take it back from the Muslims as well. When that happened, he believed, it would become possible to rebuild the Temple, which would trigger the messianic age, and his effort to find Ophir was an effort to initiate things by providing Ferdinand and Isabella with the very gold that Solomon used for his Temple.

But not everyone has been convinced that Solomon's wealth was the blessing that it appeared to be. To be sure, many biblical texts, including the description of Solomon's dream in 1 Kings 3, present material wealth as a reward that God bestows on the righteous, but some texts—including the Proverbs of Solomon—also recognize that great prosperity often has a harmful effect on those who acquire it, corrupting them, making them arrogant, or leading them into a false sense of security. This is especially true of Israel's king, who, in a passage from Deuteronomy 17 mentioned in an earlier chapter, is warned by Moses not to acquire too much gold or silver lest it turn his heart from God. Whether or not this passage was composed with Solomon in mind, its warning suggested to some readers of his story, especially rabbinic readers, that his wealth may not have been such a blessing for Solomon; it might even have contributed to his downfall.

Wealth is certainly not a blessing for Solomon's close friend Hiram, the Phoenician king of Tyre who provided the sailors for Solomon's fleet—at least as Hiram is depicted in rabbinic tradition. As depicted by the rabbis, Hiram was also a wise and wealthy king, but his good fortune has a corrupting effect on his character. As the Jewish scholar Yohanan Alemanno observed in his treatise on Solomon, great wealth makes one godlike, allowing one to influence others while making one immune to their influence in turn, and this is exactly the effect that it has on Hiram—it made him feel godlike, albeit in a negative way. So great were Hiram's pretensions to divinity, in fact, that he built a towering artificial heaven from which he presumed to preside over the earth, using some kind of machinery to simulate thunder and lightning. In an oracle recorded in Ezekiel 28 that the rabbis believed was addressed to Hiram (in midrashic tradition, Hiram, whose death is not recorded in the biblical text, continues to live into the time of the exile, making him Ezekiel's contemporary), the prophet tried to warn the king, but the Phoenician ignored him, and God then imposes a death sentence. Hiram ends up suffering an agonizing death at the hands of Nebuchadnezzar, and—in an ironic twist given Hiram's supposed interest in mining—his palace disappears into the bowels of the earth (for the sources of this tradition, see Louis Ginzberg's *The Legends of the Jews*, volume 6, note 105).

In the rabbinic reading of Solomon's story, his wealth doesn't lead him astray in quite this way, but the king himself does come to question its value. The story in question is a sequel to one that we have already mentioned. After helping Solomon build the Temple, the demon Asmodeus breaks free from the king by tricking him into handing over his magic ring; then he spits the king hundreds of miles from Jerusalem. Asmodeus claims Solomon's throne for himself, assuming his appearance, while the real Solomon embarks on a difficult three-year journey very different from the three-year journey of his ships—his punishment for having disobeyed the commandment in Deuteronomy 17 that forbade the king from acquiring too much gold and silver—and it is during this period that the king, now an outcast beggar, reflects on his former wealth and comes to regret it.

This part of Solomon's life is nowhere mentioned in 1 Kings but it does have a biblical source, the book of Ecclesiastes, which the rabbis read as a record of what happens to Solomon during his exile. Ecclesiastes was actually written centuries after Solomon, but, not knowing its real author, Jews came to attribute it to the king, partly because of the following passages, which seemed to reflect the king's great wealth:

> I was a king in Jerusalem . . . I made great works; I built houses for myself, and planted vineyards for myself. I made myself gardens and parks, and planted in them all kinds of fruit trees. I made myself pools to water the forest of sprouting trees. I bought male and female slaves, and had slaves who were born in my house as well as cattle and sheep, more than any of my predecessors in Jerusalem. I also gathered for myself silver and gold and the treasure of kings and of the provinces. [Ecclesiastes 1:12, 2:4–8]

Notice that the speaker of these verses, like Solomon, is an extremely wealthy king who has built many houses for himself and owns many possessions, including much gold and silver, but that he speaks in the past tense, as a king who has lost all his power and fortune: "I *was* a king in Jerusalem . . ." The rabbinic story of Solomon's exile, told briefly in tractate Gittin 68b, was an attempt to explain the genesis of Ecclesiastes, read as a record of what the king experienced as a poor beggar wandering from place to place.

And what has the king learned from this experience? Reduced to a life of poverty, he realizes that the Temple and all his accomplishments were for nothing: "What do people gain from all the toil at which they toil under the sun" (Ecclesiastes 1:3). In this reading, the declaration "I was king over Israel in Jerusalem" in 1:12 is what he says to those he meets during his wandering, leading them to scoff at him as a crazy homeless person. And when in 2:10 he says, "This was my reward for my toil," the "this" is a sorrowful reference to Solomon's staff—the only possession left to him.

As Solomon is going through this experience, the memory of his former fortune becomes a source of pain, but that pain also leads him to realize that there is something more valuable than material wealth. In an extension of the story told in a midrashic commentary on the book of Proverbs (*Midrash Mishle* 15, 78–79), he meets a wealthy countryman who invites him to a great feast, but he is unable to enjoy the food because the man never ceases to speak of the magnificence of Solomon's court. The next day he is invited to a meal by a poor man who could offer the king only a meager dish of vegetables, but he also offers words of comfort, reassuring him that he will one day regain his kingdom. The contrast between the two experiences is said to have inspired Solomon's observation in Proverbs 15:17: "Better is a dinner with vegetables where love is than a fatted ox and hatred with it." 1 Kings casts Solomon's wealth as a reward for his wisdom; here wisdom becomes possible only after Solomon loses all his wealth, when he can at last appreciate that the only true source of enjoyment in life is the company of other human beings.

The story of Solomon's exile is as much an interpretive invention as is the idea of Solomon's navy reaching the new world, and like other midrashic renderings of the king it projects onto him the rabbis' own experiences. In the rabbinic culture out of which this story emerged, the sage often had to leave his wife and livelihood behind and travel great distances to his places of study, suffering loneliness and impoverishment along the way. Some sages like Hillel are remembered in the Talmud as suffering severe financial hardship to pursue their studies. Others gave up great fortunes to pursue this kind of life. A rabbi named Eleazar ben Harsom, for example, was so wealthy that he owned a thousand ships, and yet each day he would take a flask of flour on his shoulder and wander from town to town to study Torah (both stories appear in b. *Yoma* 35b). The story of Solomon's exile transforms him into this kind of sage by using Ecclesiastes to imagine for the king a period of exile and privation through which he is forced to see wealth from the outside looking in. Like those who coveted the riches of Solomon, the rabbis found between the lines of the biblical text the story of a great journey, but it is a journey not toward wealth but away from it, from a life of prosperity to the more difficult and—in the rabbis' view—more worthwhile life to which they themselves were committed.

This interpretation, too, reads much into the biblical text, which nowhere suggests that there was anything regrettable about Solomon's wealth. But neither is there anything in the text that rules out this reading; to the contrary, while the Bible depicts wealth as a blessing, it also recognizes that it can be a curse. "The reward for humility and fear of the Lord is riches and honor and life," says Solomon at one point in Proverbs (22:4)—but elsewhere he notes, "Those who trust in their riches will fall" (11:28). The truth is that Solomon's wealth, like so many other aspects of his life, is irresolvably open-ended.

The ancients did develop one way of assessing the benefits of wealth that we might apply here—observe what happened to the rich over the course of their lives. Did it actually improve their lives or only increase their sorrows in the end? As King Croesus, that other great tycoon of antiquity, learned after losing all his wealth, call no man fortunate until the day he dies. But even that measure doesn't help us because the end of Solomon's life is ambiguous in its own right: Ecclesiastes might register his final experiences, or not; Solomon might have regretted his wealth, or not. There is much one might learn by pinning the king's life down to one possibility or the other—the king's story might show that one can be rich and a good person at the same time as many biblical self-help books contend, or it might show the opposite, that the acquisition of wealth is spiritually harmful—but the Bible is too equivocal to allow us to draw conclusions, and the wisdom we would need to resolve its ambiguities lies, for better or worse, in the same uncharitable region where Ophir itself still waits to be discovered.

9

Difficult Questions from a Dubious Queen

For those readers who wonder whether Solomon really was as wise and as rich as the Bible claims, 1 Kings offers a most authoritative eyewitness: the Queen of Sheba. The Queen has traveled a great distance, arriving with a retinue of camels bearing spices, gold, and precious stones, but the purpose of her visit is not simply to honor the king but to see for herself if what she has heard about Solomon's wisdom is true by testing him with a series of difficult questions. She is no fool herself—she alone questions the king's public image—but King Solomon proves smarter still, answering all her questions, so that in the end she too acknowledges the superiority of his understanding: "Happy are your servants, the ones who tend to you, and who always get to hear your wisdom" (1 Kings 10:8).

The Queen was just one of many rulers who visits Solomon to hear his wisdom, but no other ruler merits the same attention, and this raises the question this chapter will try to answer: What was it about the Queen that distinguishes her from all the other rulers who pay their respects to Solomon? Is there something about her that merits special mention? Neither Kings nor Chronicles answers these questions directly, but in the centuries after the Bible was written Jews, Christians, and Muslims retold her story in ways that fill in the Bible's gaps. Their versions of the Queen are fantastical, turning her into a figure worthy of the *Arabian Nights*, but they also register instructive literary intuitions that may help us to understand why the biblical authors describe her visit in such detail.

One possible reason that the biblical text—and Solomon himself, for that matter—take such an interest in the Queen, these sources suggest, is her sex appeal. In the biblical versions of the tale, Solomon and the Queen only exchange gifts and a bit of conversation, nothing more, but Jewish and Muslim interpreters imagined the Queen as an extraordinarily beautiful woman (or as a demoness disguised as a beautiful woman) and retold her encounter with Solomon as a story of seduction or love, an image of the Queen that survives into our own day thanks to Hollywood, which has long counted on the Queen's sex appeal to sell tickets. Even before her first appearance on the silver screen, the Queen was the star of burlesque spectacles like one produced by the Ringling Brothers and that featured a beauty from their hometown of Baraboo, Wisconsin. Hollywood continued that tradition by casting a long line of scantily clad starlets as the Queen: the vampish Betty Blythe in William Fox's *Queen of Sheba* from 1921 (the film itself has been lost but an image of Ms. Blythe as the Queen remains); the Italian actress Leonora Ruffo in 1951's *The Queen of Sheba*; another, more famous Italian, Gina Lollobrigida, in the 1959 *Solomon and Sheba* (an ill-fated production whose original Solomon, Tyrone Power, died of a heart attack while rehearsing a sword fight with Adonijah); and, most recently, Halle Berry in a 1995 television movie by the same name.

The actress Betty Blythe enthroned as the Queen of Sheba (1921).
(Reprinted with permission from mptvimages)

But is it the Queen's sexuality that drew the biblical authors to give her so much attention? Possibly, but their accounts do not seem to treat her as a sex object in the way later movie makers did, never describing what she looks like or mentioning that she is beautiful, much less reporting anything overtly sexual about her encounter with the king.

Perhaps, then, it is not her sex appeal but her exotic background that distinguishes the Queen, who seems to travel a great distance to reach Jerusalem. Both Jewish and Muslim interpreters assumed that the kingdom of Sheba was exceptionally far away, some putting it in known places like Yemen, others locating it even farther away. In a story appearing both in the Quran and in Jewish sources, Solomon learns of Sheba from a hoopoe, a bird that is able to fly to those parts of the world that the king cannot reach. The land where he finds the Queen, according to one source, lies far in the east, and the hoopoe's description makes it sound like the Garden of Eden itself—its dust is more precious than gold, and its trees are watered by the rivers of paradise. In some versions of the Solomon story, the king does eventually make it to Sheba himself but only because he possesses a magic carpet able to travel great distances. He makes the trip not on the single-seater that one imagines Aladdin riding but on miles of wind-propelled green silk transporting not just the king but his entire retinue and even his throne. Traversing the distances between Syria and Afghanistan in the time that separates breakfast from dinner, the carpet made it possible for Solomon to construct buildings in far-flung places like Persia, and it enabled him to visit the Queen on a regular basis. To travel the other way, on the other hand, the Queen had to ride a camel—a journey that, according to one source, took three years, which was less than the seven years that such a journey normally required.

Christian tradition would place the Queen in other exotic locales, well beyond the Middle East. In the New Testament she is known as the "Queen of the South," *regina austri* in the Latin translation, which helps to explain why some explorers thought Solomon's gold was to be found in an unknown southern continent, the *Terra Australis Incognita*. Identifying this place with the kingdom of Sheba, they assumed that it must be in the unexplored southern hemisphere, in southern African or the South Pacific. The latter location was where Álvaro de Mendaña de Neira was looking, for example, when in 1568 he came across the archipelago now known as the Solomon Islands. The Queen's association with this southern region helps to explain a curious incident that occurred after Álvaro died during a failed attempt to return to the islands. Upon his death his wife, Isabel Barreto, whose father had sought the source of Solomon's gold in Africa, took command of the fleet and, despite the loss of many sailors to sickness and a resentful pilot who thought he should be in charge, was able to lead her ships to safety in Manila. When the people there heard that a powerful woman was in command (Isabel, incidentally, may be the first woman in history to serve as an admiral), and that she had just arrived from the isles of Solomon, they hailed her as the Queen of Sheba herself.

The Bible itself does not seem particularly interested in where the Queen comes from, however, nor does it make her any more exotic than the other rulers who pay their respects to the king. There is no indication in Kings or Chronicles that the Queen traveled farther than others to see the king, nor is there any suggestion that her homeland is especially mysterious or unusual. In fact, many interpreters place it much closer to Jerusalem. Josephus, for example, makes the Queen a ruler of Egypt, and more recent scholars believe that Sheba abutted Solomon's kingdom in the Negev desert or northern Arabia. These are all plausible possibilities because the biblical accounts simply do not give any geographical information about where she came from other than to imply (by noting her retinue of camels) that she had probably traveled across a desert to reach Jerusalem.

What really seems to distinguish the Queen from Solomon's other visitors is not her sexual attractiveness or her exotic background; rather, it is her skepticism, her reluctance to believe what she cannot see with her own eyes or personally examine. Of all the rulers who hear of Solomon's wisdom, she alone questions what she has heard: "I did not believe the reports," she explains to the king, and it is only after he answers all her questions and she personally tours his palace with its well-stocked table and well-dressed servants—in other words, only after she sees things with her own eyes—that she becomes convinced that the king is as wise and as wealthy as people claim that he is: "I did not believe the reports *until I came, and my own eyes have seen it*" (1 Kings 10:7).

Although we do not know what she looks like or even what her name is, the Queen's need for corroboration makes her one of the most empathetic figures in Solomon's story, certainly far easier to relate to than the king himself. He has no need for evidence or cross-examination to distinguish between true reports and false ones, as we saw in our consideration of his judgment, which is what makes his wisdom seem so inhuman, while the impulse that drives her is not unlike the one that drives our own quest for Solomon—we are not sure what to believe, and we want to see things for ourselves. Perhaps, then, the author of 1 Kings gives more attention to the Queen than to any other of Solomon's visitors because he knows that we will recognize ourselves in her; her mind wants to know the secret of things but does so in the limited way our minds do, without the illumination of divine wisdom, confined to the realm of observable experience.

But then Solomon answers all her questions; her doubts are resolved and at that moment the Queen passes from our world into Solomon's, leaving us alone with our unanswered questions. Not only are we unable to know anything certain about Solomon, in fact, but if we were to operate according to the Queen's criterion of credibility, if the only reports that we believe are the ones we can confirm with our own eyes, then we would need to question her existence as well since we cannot verify any of the Bible's claims about his or her kingdom. Not that scholars haven't tried to figure out who she was and where she came from; their efforts simply have yielded no insights into the historical Queen. In just the past fifteen years, there have been not one but two attempts to find her kingdom, one based in Ethiopia, another in Yemen, but neither has been able to produce the kind of clear-cut corroborating evidence that the Queen would demand.

In Ethiopia, where the Queen is known as Makeda, the story is told that during her visit to Jerusalem Solomon tricked her into having sex with him and fathered a son named Menelik. It was this son who would go on to found a dynasty that ruled Ethiopia from its capital in Axum. The official version of this story is the epic *Kebra Nagast*, written in the early fourteenth century, but it may go back much further, and decades after the death of Haile Selassie in 1975, the last of their line, she retains her stature in Ethiopia, a ubiquitous presence in art, advertising, and souvenir shops. Ethiopians, incidentally, are not the only ones to accept this version of the Queen's story. The crowning of Haile Selassie as emperor of Ethiopia in 1930 was an internationally reported event, and his rule had particular impact on a Jamaican minister named Leonard Howell, who proclaimed him a messianic figure. Howell's followers, known as Rastafarians in honor of Selassie's royal name Ras Tafari, accept him as a descendant of Solomon and the Queen. The best known Rastafarian in history, the reggae singer Bob Marley, named his daughter Makeda, and his widow, Rita, owns an Ethiopian restaurant in Kingston, Jamaica, called *The Queen of Sheba*—all reverberations of how Ethiopians remember the Queen.

But another country is no less confident in its claim to be the Queen's homeland—Yemen in the south. There she is known as Bilqis—the name bestowed on her in Islamic tradition (the name may be derived from the Hebrew for concubine, *pilegesh*, or else may represent a garbled form of the name known to Josephus, Nikaulis) and her identification as the Queen of Yemen also goes way back, deriving from her association with the "South," which is the meaning of the word *Yemen* in Arabic. Islamic legend claims that Solomon visited the Queen in Yemen on a monthly basis and established several forts there, and sites associated with the Queen exist to this day, especially the "Throne of Bilqis" and the *Mahram Bilqis*, the "Sacred Place of Bilqis," both in Marib, an ancient city that Yemenis believe was the capital of her kingdom.

Whichever of these two countries can convincingly claim to be the home of the Queen of Sheba has a lot to gain, in terms of both prestige and tourism, and thus both have sought to enlist archaeologists to provide the kind of evidence that can convince skeptical foreigners. In 1997, Yemen allowed archaeologists under the auspices of the American Foundation for the Study of Man to excavate the *Mahram Bilqis*, while in 1999 an archaeologist from the University of Hamburg, with the support of the Ethiopian Ministry for Culture, began seeking evidence of the Queen in the vicinity of Axum.

But neither of these excavations has been able to shed any light on the Queen herself, one claiming to have made great discoveries that seem entirely illusory, the other being more modest in its claims but reaching no certain conclusions. The German team in Axum already claims to have discovered the Queen's palace, and at one point seemed on the verge of announcing the discovery of the ark itself (which, according to Ethiopian tradition, was smuggled out of Jerusalem by Menelik and relocated to Axum), but their methods are so suspect that even the former head of Ethiopian Studies at the University of Hamburg itself, Siegbert Uhlig, has felt it necessary to issue a press release that renounces the effort. By that standard, the excavation at Merab seems a much more responsible undertaking—Yemen has long been favored by scholars as the probable site of Sheba because an ancient kingdom with the similar name of Saba once existed there, and this kingdom was known for its trade in spices—one of the gifts that the Queen presents to Solomon. The excavation there has yet to find any direct evidence of the Queen herself, however, and its director admits that such a discovery is unlikely.

Absent any evidence outside the Bible, we have no way to answer any of our questions about the Queen. As it happens, however, many of the stories told of the Queen in Jewish and Muslim sources themselves argue for a different view of how to ascertain the truth. Over and against the biblical Queen's insistence on seeing things for herself, these later traditions celebrate another kind of insight that they associate with Solomon's transcendent wisdom, a way of ascertaining the truth that does not depend on sense perception. Solomon's ability to resolve the case of the two mothers, where it should have been impossible to determine the truth, is the most famous example of this insight, but the king puts it on display again during the Queen's visit, using it to answer her questions. In Jewish and Muslim tradition, these questions are remembered as riddles, and not just difficult riddles but ones that were often impossible to resolve, and Solomon's ability to solve them is understood to mean, in contradiction to what the Queen represents, that there are ways of ascertaining the truth that go beyond what we can see with our eyes.

The Bible itself does not describe the content of the Queen's questions—this was a detail filled in by later interpreters, and they did so in light of how the riddle was understood to function in antiquity. Some believed she asked abstruse philosophical or scientific questions: What is God like?

Is the visible world all that there is? What is the source of wisdom? More commonly, however, Jews and Muslims reconstructed her riddles on the basis of how that genre was understood in a classical Greek tradition of riddle-telling to which they were heir. The ancient Greeks loved to tell stories about riddles and their solutions. The most famous example is the story of how Oedipus solved the riddle of the Sphinx; it is one of scores of examples, and we know that this kind of story had an influence on Jews from a very early period. Josephus, in fact, recounts the story of a riddle contest between Solomon and Hiram that is very similar to Greek riddle stories from the same period (*Against Apion* 1.113–15), and rabbinic sources from a few centuries later record riddle contests between the Jews and the Athenians. Part of what made such stories so popular is that they offered a way for peoples to assert their intellectual superiority—for the Greeks to show they were smarter than barbarians, for the Jews to show that they were smarter than the Greeks. In the story that Josephus recounts about Solomon and Hiram, interestingly, it is Hiram who eventually wins when he enlists a sage named Abdemon to compose riddles that Solomon cannot answer, but this is probably because the story originated not from Josephus himself but from among the Phoenicians as an attempt to show that they were even smarter than the Jews.

What made riddle-solving the ultimate demonstration of intellectual prowess? For the Greeks, the ability to solve a riddle was the ability to answer a question that doesn't seem to have a solution. Often the riddle collapses the distinction between opposites like animal and plant or male and female, and the answer thus appears to be something, to paraphrase Aristotle's definition of the genre, that is "impossibly true"—in other words, a riddle will seem to refer to something that cannot exist and yet does. A good riddle in this tradition is one that most people cannot answer because it seems to have no solution, and the ability to solve a riddle is for that reason considered an almost supernatural feat akin to divination or prophecy.

This, according to Jewish and Muslim tradition, is the kind of riddle that the Queen asks Solomon, a riddle that seems impossibly true, as in the following example: "Alive, it does not move; when its head is cut off, it moves. What is it?" This riddle—one that the Queen posed to Solomon according to a medieval Jewish source known as *Midrash Ha-hefez*—seems to describe something that contradicts the laws of science, overturning our sense of what distinguishes life from death. The answer is the wood used to make a boat—so long as the wood was part of a living tree, it could not move. The answer makes perfect sense once it has been revealed by the riddle-asker but is exceedingly difficult to figure out on one's own because it has been cleverly concealed by an act of linguistic misdirection: one has to figure out that the word "head" is really a metaphor for a treetop. One cannot solve such a riddle by going out in the world in search of evidence, as the Queen journeys to Jerusalem to verify the reports she heard about Solomon, or as archaeologists travel to seek out proof of the Queen's existence. One solves the riddle only by *not* believing one's eyes—by distrusting appearances, and by discerning what lies hidden behind them.

This, according to Jewish and Islamic tradition, is the skill that Solomon draws on to answer the Queen's difficult riddles. 1 Kings reports that the king answered all of the Queen's questions, but it does not tell us what they consisted of; later Jewish and Muslim sources sought to fill in the content of those riddles, and added to them other challenges designed to test Solomon's ability to detect things he cannot see directly. In one source, for instance, the Queen lines up some young children before the king, with the boys dressed as girls and the girls dressed as boys, and asks him to identify their gender. This was impossible to determine based on their appearance alone, but

Solomon was able to do so by throwing nuts before the children and noting their response. Some simply grabbed the nuts while others first put on gloves, and Solomon correctly reasoned that the latter were the girls because of their greater modesty. In another story recounted by the medieval Muslim scholar Al-Talabi, the Queen presents the king with a box and asks him to tell her what is inside without opening it, and the king is able to do so by consulting an angel.

To appreciate Solomon's extraordinary ability to solve these kinds of challenges, it is helpful to contrast them with the Queen's response when, as Jews and Muslims tell her story, the king tests her in a similar way. The episode in question goes back to the Quran, the most sacred text of Islam, appearing in Sura 27. The story is more alluded to than told, and it is a little hard to follow, but what seems to happen is that Solomon, seeking to learn whether the Queen is "truly guided"—that is, guided by divine wisdom as he himself is—stages a test that involves the magnificent throne from which she rules. That throne, of course, is very far away and extremely difficult to move—it is eighty cubits in length and height and locked away behind a series of locked gates to which only the Queen has the key—but Solomon is able to make it appear in his court in the "twinkling of an eye" with the help of a mysterious figure referred to only as "the one who had knowledge of the book"— probably an angel or maybe a demon. The test that Solomon has in mind is to see whether the Queen will recognize the throne as her own, a challenge that the king makes even more difficult by ordering his servants to change its appearance.

When the Queen arrives and is shown the throne, it instantly looks familiar to her, but she knows that it cannot be her throne—it is simply impossible for it to be there—and so, when asked by the king if she recognizes it, her response is equivocal: "It is as if it were." How different this is from Solomon's response to a similarly impossible intellectual challenge: "She is his mother," he says unambiguously. The Queen's response is very shrewd, finding an answer that is neither true nor false, but as smart as it is, it still reflects the limits of the human mind, suspicious of appearances but unable to get beyond them, whereas Solomon's wisdom, a perfect wisdom learned from angels, demons, and God, can resolve any ambiguity, penetrate any secret. If the king had been faced with this challenge, he would have answered correctly without hesitation or self-doubt; the Queen can only hedge her bets, and this is why she fails the test.

If we had the riddle-solving ability of King Solomon, we would be able to answer our many questions about the Queen —to figure out what she looked like, where she was from, and what she asked the king—but of course our situation is much closer to that of the Queen herself. The experience of reading her story is analogous to the Queen's challenge in trying to recognize her throne; we might come close to guessing the truth, but we can never be sure because we are human—we can sometimes sense things that lie beyond our comprehension but we cannot quite grasp or understand them, and in the end the biblical text is a riddle we cannot solve. But this very predicament is proof of Solomon's extraordinary status: there will always be gaps in our understanding whereas, in the words of 1 Kings 10:3, "nothing is hidden" from Solomon; he alone can understand things that are "impossibly true," and that is why, the biblical narrative seems to be implying, we too must submit to him and the divine wisdom that he represents.

Thus it is that the Queen of Sheba became an exemplary figure in Jewish, Muslim, and Christian tradition. She is a symbol of the mind's resistance to divine revelation—the intellectual independence, the skepticism, the need for physical proof that makes it difficult for a reasoning mind to submit to the authority of religion, which is rooted in unsolvable riddles and impossible truths—and the fact that she is vanquished in the end, forced to acknowledge Solomon's superior wisdom, was seen as an example for those who might have their doubts about God. But as someone not quite ready to submit himself, what I also find interesting about the story of the Queen of Sheba—not the biblical story, but the story as retold in later religious tradition—is that it also sometimes registers anxiety about the kind of all-knowing, transrational certitude that Solomon represents, recognizing something dangerous in his capacity to answer every riddle.

An example is a medieval version of the story preserved in a text known as the *Alphabet of Ben Sira*. The original Ben Sira was a sage from the Second Temple period and was known as the author of a book of wisdom similar to the book of Proverbs, but in the *Alphabet of Ben Sira* he is a young child ordered to appear before Nebuchadnezzar, who has heard about his precocious wisdom and is so intent on learning it himself that he is willing to threaten and torture Ben Sira to extract his secrets. Notice that the Babylonian here plays the part of the Queen to Ben Sira's Solomon—he is the asker of difficult questions—and as the text eventually discloses, the resemblance is no accident.

One of the things that Nebuchadnezzar is curious about is a special shaving cream invented by Ben Sira. The child had used it to remove the hair from a pet rabbit—this was before the age of razors—and the king was curious to know how he managed such a smooth shave. A bit of a smart aleck, Ben Sira responds that he should ask his own mother. "How would she know?" the king responds. Ben Sira then gives an account of how the cream was invented, which turns out to be the story of Solomon and the Queen of Sheba. During her visit to Jerusalem, Solomon found her to be very beautiful and wanted to have sex with her, Ben Sira explains, but she was also very hairy, and this repelled him. In other versions of the Queen of Sheba legend, the Queen's hairy legs were a sign that she was really a demon or half-demon, and for this reason she keeps them concealed under a long dress. In those stories, the focus is on how

Solomon tricks her into revealing her true identity by using a ruse—a glass floor designed to look like a pool of water—to fool her into lifting her skirt. Here, the king concentrates his wisdom on the problem of how to persuade the Queen to remove the hair, which she is reluctant to do because of the pain of shaving, and he solves the problem by inventing a depilatory, a lotion that can remove hair without a blade. This answers Nebuchadnezzar's question, but why would his mother be in a position to know the answer? After the Queen removes the hair from her legs, Solomon consents to have sex with her; she becomes pregnant, and her child is none other than Nebuchadnezzar himself. She is his mother.

Solomon's solution to the problem of the Queen's hairy legs, as unremarkable as that might now seem in this age of disposable safety razors, reflects the same kind of uncanny skill that he used to solve the Queen's riddles. Like the riddle, the Queen's hairy legs, a supposedly male trait on a female body, collapses the distinction between opposite categories (as those categories were defined before feminism challenged them) but Solomon, as one might expect, resolves the ambiguity in a way no one else can figure out. Another victory for the king's divine wisdom except, in this instance, Solomon's riddle-solving ability leads to tragic consequences when it produces Nebuchadnezzar, the ruler who destroys the Temple and everything else that Solomon achieves.

Why does the *Alphabet of Ben Sira* choose to end the story of Solomon and the Queen of Sheba in this way? It is certainly possible that its author is trying to warn his readers, presumably young male Jewish students, against having sex with foreign women—this is not the only episode in the work in which a character has sex with the wrong kind of woman—but I cannot resist the thought that the story also conveys a lesson about the danger of being able to solve every problem. Perfect knowledge certainly puts Solomon at an advantage over those like the Queen who can understand the world only imperfectly, but, precisely because nothing lies beyond its power, this wisdom has the potential to become despotic, in this version of Solomon's story actually spawning a despot. The imperiousness of such a mind is not fully manifest in the Solomon of the *Alphabet of Ben Sira* though there, disturbingly, he seems to force himself onto the Queen, but it certainly comes into the open through Nebuchadnezzar, whose cruelty directly descends from a Solomonic ambition to know everything.

This is by no means the only way to end the story of Solomon and the Queen of Sheba—in Ethiopia, as we have noted, her son goes on to establish the ruling dynasty of the country, and in other traditions, she remains a virgin her entire life, becoming a prototype for Mary mother of Jesus—but the ending in the *Alphabet of Ben Sira* sticks with me, I think, because of the questions it raises about our own efforts to solve the riddles of the biblical account. It is frustrating not to know who the Queen really was, where she came from, or what transpired between her and Solomon, but reaching such knowledge—as the quixotic quests of recent archaeology remind us—requires something more than the limited puzzle-solving skills of scholars; one would need the unrestrained understanding of Solomon, the kind that does not permit anything to be hidden from it. Even if it were possible to acquire such knowledge, however, the tragic aftermath of the king's riddle-solving ability in the *Alphabet of Ben Sira* makes me wonder whether being able to answer all of our questions in a Solomonic way might trigger its own destructive backlash; perhaps it is better, after all, that there be riddles no one but Solomon can solve.

10

A Thousand and One Sex Scandals

DESPITE THE EFFORTS of later interpreters to turn his encounter with the Queen of Sheba into an amorous relationship,
Solomon as he is described in 1 Kings 1–10 does not seem to
have had much of a sex life. His father David had a very active
libido—it is what got him in trouble with Bathsheba—but
1 Kings does not detail any such love stories or sexual scandals
for Solomon. The one sexual relationship disclosed to us prior
to 1 Kings 11 is his marriage to the daughter of Pharaoh, who,
in contrast to Davidic wives like Abigail, Michal, and Bathsheba, is never given a story of her own, a story that attends in
some way to her perspective on things, or even so much as
named, and Solomon's decision to marry her seems more a political act than a personal one, a way of formalizing his kingdom's new alliance with Egypt. In later tradition, Solomon
would be remembered as the author of the most passionate
book in the Bible, the Song of Songs, but for most of the ac-

count in 1 Kings he doesn't seem the type to sing love songs, coming across as unimpassioned—devoid of desire or any feelings, for that matter.

But then we reach the final chapter of Solomon's life, 1 Kings 11, and at that moment it suddenly becomes clear that the narrative has been holding back on us:

> King Solomon loved many foreign women—the daughter of Pharaoh, Moabite women, Ammonite women, Edomite women, Sidonian women and Hittite women, from the nations concerning which the Lord has said to the Israelites, "You shall not come unto them [a biblical euphemism for sexual relations] or they you; for they will lead your heart to follow their gods." To these Solomon clutched in love.
> [1 Kings 11:1–2]

Far from being a passionless king, Solomon, it turns out, seems to have a much stronger libido than his father or, arguably, any other king, for that matter. We know of other rulers who had large harems. The Egyptian Ramses II, best known as the likely pharaoh of the Exodus story, was the father of close to two hundred children (this was discovered after someone named a brand of condoms for him), which implies dozens, perhaps scores, of wives and concubines but nowhere close to a thousand. The famous harems of the Ottoman Empire, even at their heyday in the sixteenth and seventeenth centuries, were sometimes populated by up to a thousand people, but this number included not just wives and concubines but the Sultan's daughters and hundreds of staff and servants. It would seem that Solomon conducted his sex life on the same unmatchable scale that he did everything else.

In fact, it is scarcely possible to conceive a sex life on this scale. In 1921 the Yiddish writer David Pinski tried, undertaking an audacious attempt to describe all 1,000 of Solomon's wives, but though he worked for fifteen years he managed to complete portraits of only 105; there were just too many to handle—and he was merely writing about them. Solomon seems to do everything in multiples of thousands—40,000 stalls for his horses; 180,000 laborers to build the Temple; a sacrifice consisting of 22,000 oxen and 120,000 sheep—but no figure in 1 Kings has impressed itself on the imagination, or strains it, quite like the king's 700 wives and 300 concubines.

If the historical Solomon really did have a large harem, he was probably quite proud of it. Biblical family values allowed a man to have multiple wives and concubines (it was only in the Middle Ages that Jews embraced monogamy as the ideal), and a large family was considered a mark of virility, wealth, blessing—evidence that a man was favored by God. In the *Kebra Nagast*, the Ethiopian version of Solomon's story, the king's motive for marrying so many women is a pious one; he wants to fulfill God's promise to Israel of many descendants more numerous than the stars in the sky, and there seemed to him no better way to help bring this about than to have sex with as many women as possible (including, in this instance, the Queen of Sheba). For an ancient ruler, marriage was also a useful diplomatic tool. Marrying the daughter of another ruler was a way of strengthening one's alliance with that ruler, interweaving the futures of the two kingdoms, and also, implicitly, securing a valuable hostage in case relations soured. What we know of royal marriages in the ancient Near East makes it quite plausible to suppose that many of Solomon's wives, like the daughter of Pharaoh, were foreign princesses given to him to seal a treaty, in which case their large number signified not only the king's extraordinary virility and wealth but also his exceptional well-connectedness.

The author of 1 Kings was far from impressed, however. To him, Solomon's marriages were his fatal mistake, the act that ruined everything. The problem was not the number of women that he married but who they were. We are told virtually nothing about Solomon's wives as individuals—only one is given a name, Naamah, the mother of Solomon's successor Rehoboam, and only because she was the mother of a future king. What 1 Kings does make a point of revealing, however, is the ethnic background of these women—they were Moabites, Ammonites, Edomites, Sidonians, and Hittites, non-Israelite peoples who lived within or on the borders of the land of Canaan—and that is what doomed Solomon's marriages to them from the start.

The Bible does not prohibit intermarriage per se—it would probably have been permissible for Solomon to marry an Ethiopian as Moses did, for example, and perhaps it was even religiously acceptable for him to marry the daughter of Pharaoh. The women from the nations listed in 1 Kings 11 were off-limits, however, because they were Canaanites, the peoples who lived in the land before Israel's arrival. God had decided to expel these nations because their idolatrous ways were having a corrupting effect on the land, and it was Israel's responsibility to carry out the purge—to destroy their altars and idols, to kill or expel the Canaanites themselves, and to erase their memory from the place. Since the Israelites are not able to eliminate them all at once, in the meantime they are to avoid interaction, especially intermarriage: "Do not marry them! Do not give your daughter to their son, or take their daughter for your son, for that would turn away your children from after me, and they will serve other gods" (Deuteronomy 7:3–4). This sin is precisely the one that Solomon commits in 1 Kings 11, and the result, as Moses predicts, is that he is led astray, turned from God to the gods of other nations:

> In the time of Solomon's old age, his wives led his heart astray after other gods, and his heart was not full with the Lord his God as the heart of David his father. And Solomon went after Ashtarot, the god of the Sidonians; and after Milcom, the abomination of the Ammonites. And Solomon did

evil in the eyes of the Lord, and he was not completely loyal to the Lord as David his father. It was then that Solomon built a shrine for Kemosh, the abomination of Moab on the mountain across from Jerusalem [probably the Mount of Olives], and for Molech the abomination of the Ammonites, and thus he did for all his foreign wives who offered incense and made sacrifices to their gods. [1 Kings 11:4–8]

It was bad enough to violate the law on marrying Canaanite women, but Solomon went further: worshiping other gods was the worst possible sin that an Israelite could commit. David committed his share of serious offenses, including adultery and murder, but the one transgression that trumped all these other sins was idolatry, for it betrayed the relationship with God, upon which all the rest of the Torah's laws were premised.

Which brings us to one of the most difficult questions posed by the life of Solomon: how is it that the wisest man in the world, the pious builder of the Temple, could have sinned, much less commit the worst possible offense against God? His wisdom was supposed to teach him how to distinguish good from evil, truth from falsehood, and he should thus have understood that the worship of other gods was not just a violation of a divine command but also an act of folly, a mistaking of a falsehood as a truth, and Solomon of all people should have been able to avoid such a mistake. Indeed, according to the *Wisdom of Solomon*—a work that many Christians believe was written by Solomon—the king did know better, warning others against the folly of idolatry: "The idea of making idols was the beginning of fornication, and the invention of them was the corruption of life; for they did not exist from the beginning, nor will they last forever. For through human vanity they entered the world, and therefore their speedy end has been planned" (*Wisdom of Solomon* 14:12–14). That one who knew such things could fall into idolatry himself is deeply perplexing. If wisdom was what the philosophers said it was—if it was supposed to reveal the true nature of things—how could the wisest of sages have gotten things so wrong?

This problem is so disturbing that many interpreters have looked for ways to exonerate Solomon. By now, the reader will not be surprised to learn that the Chronicler simply eliminated the episode of Solomon's sin, and there have always been religious authorities willing to simply ignore what he did: such was the view of the third century sage Rabbi Shmuel bar Nachmani, for example, quoted in the Babylonian Talmud as speaking in the name of Rabbi Yonatan: "Whoever says that Solomon sinned is mistaken" (*Shabbat* 56a). The rabbi seems to be blatantly ignoring 1 Kings 11, but his reading is probably based on another of those small textual oddities in the Hebrew text that is invisible in English translation. In 1 King 11:7—"Then Solomon built a shrine to Kemosh"—the verb "built" is in the past tense, but only when read in context and in the light of what we now know about the grammar of biblical Hebrew. Without that knowledge, the verb (*yivneh*) appears in a tense used to describe actions not yet completed—in other words, its form allows it to be understood as "he was going to build" or "he would have built." Read literally in this way, the text can be construed as saying that while Solomon intended to commit idolatry, he didn't necessarily act on the impulse.

Other interpreters seized on another detail in 1 Kings to exonerate the king. 1 Kings nowhere actually says that Solomon believed in or worshiped other gods himself. He enables others to worship them by building shrines, but he isn't depicted making sacrifices to them or praying to them as he does with the Lord, leaving open the possibility that he was simply going along with his wives' practices and never believed in their gods himself or, in other words, that his sin was not committing idolatry himself but merely enabling his wives to do so. According to another view recorded in the Babylonian Talmud, for example, the king's mistake was not to protest against his wives' behavior, a sin of omission counted against him as if he sinned himself but not the same as believing in false gods (*Shabbat* 56b). Not a defense exactly, but it salvages the king's reputation for wisdom, since his error in this reading is not an intellectual one, mistaking false gods as real, but a sin of being an enabler, abetting his wives in the fulfillment of their desires.

Even if one was inclined to exonerate Solomon of the charge of idolatry, however, that did not solve the larger problem that Solomon's sin posed, the problem of how such a wise person could do such a foolish thing. If the rabbis were correct that his wisdom included understanding of the Torah, he should surely have known Deuteronomy 17, which in addition to prohibiting the king from trading horses with Egypt and acquiring too much gold and silver, also warned him against marrying too many women: "He must not acquire many wives for himself, or else his heart will turn away" (in the light of this passage, interestingly, it is not the foreignness of Solomon's wives that makes it problematic to marry them, but their quantity, the fact that he acquired too many women just as he acquired too much wealth). A king who understood Torah better than anyone else must have known this law, so how could Solomon have disregarded it?

There is more at stake in this question than simply understanding how Solomon himself went awry. What makes wisdom worth wanting in the first place—whether one defines wisdom as philosophical insight, scientific knowledge, or the understanding of the Torah and its laws—is that it is supposed to make one a better and happier person, but this is not what happens to Solomon. As the wisest man in the world, he should have been the most virtuous and most contented, and yet in his final years, he seems a complete fool, succumbing to desire, endorsing beliefs he should have known to be false. What happened to all his knowledge? Why didn't it prevent him from making such terrible mistakes? And what does his downfall say about wisdom itself? Is it wrong to assume that wisdom makes one a better person, as both biblical and Greek sages claimed? The end of Solomon's life not only discredits the king; it also potentially discredits wisdom itself with the example that calls into question the philosopher's equation of understanding with self-restraint, virtuous behavior, and happiness.

Secular biblical scholarship does not help us to answer such questions, but it does make it easier to ignore them. During World War II, a German scholar named Martin Noth proposed that the books of Deuteronomy through 2 Kings constituted a single work composed by a single anonymous author that Noth referred to as the Deuteronomistic Historian, a scholar who lived sometime after the Babylonian exile in 586 B.C.E. and who wrote this work in order to explain why God had permitted such a catastrophe to befall Israel. The Deuteronomistic Historian did not work from scratch, incorporating earlier sources into his work, but he rearranged everything very carefully and added much material in order to develop what amounts to a devastating critique of the Israelite monarchy—in his view, a presumptuous, abusive, and easily corrupted institution that God had never wanted in the first place and which led the people to violate the laws of Moses. The description of Solomon's sins in 1 Kings 11 is part of this critique, reflecting one of the telltale signs of the Deuteronomistic Historian's editorial style by alluding to Deuteronomic law—the prohibition against intermarriage with the Canaanites. If the transition from Solomon's accomplishments to his sins seems abrupt, if his idolatry seems to contradict his wisdom, this is because the story in 1 Kings 11 originated independent of most of the material in 1 Kings 1–10, reflecting the perspective of a later editor who blamed kings like Solomon for the Babylonian exile.

This view has much to recommend it—and it would explain what seems like a very puzzling inconsistency in Solomon's behavior—but it is, in the end, only a theory, and there are problems with it. As successful as modern scholarship has been in sorting out the pro-Solomon parts of the story from the anti-Solomon parts in 1 Kings 1–11, for example, there is much in this account that cannot be neatly categorized in one way or the other, qualities in Solomon that can be read as either virtues or vices, aspects of his life that can be read as blessings or as the prelude to his downfall. We have seen this again and again throughout this book: Is his alliance with the king of Egypt a fulfillment of God's promise to make Solomon more honored than any other ruler, or is it a hint that he is undoing the Exodus? Is Solomon's great wealth a fulfillment of God's promise to make the king richer than any other or a violation of the law in Deuteronomy 17, which prohibits Israel's kings from acquiring too much gold and silver? This ambiguity is an aspect of the portrait of Solomon in 1 Kings that modern scholars have not been able to figure out fully, resisting their impulse to sort reality into clear-cut categories.

It did not occur to premodern readers of the Bible that they could resolve tensions like this one by breaking the narrative down into sources written in different historical periods. In their view, of course, 1 Kings told a single, coherent story: if Solomon's behavior seemed surprising and inconsistent—if it was hard to understand how a king gifted with divine wisdom could fall into the worship of false gods—there had to be an explanation somewhere in his biography, perhaps not directly recorded in the biblical text but inferable from the hints or clues that it was thought to provide. To revive such a view in the twenty-first century would seem incredibly naïve—ignoring all the evidence that led scholars to detect multiple sources in 1 Kings 1–11—but because it does not so easily explain away the inconsistencies in Solomon's character, it also allows for a more complex Solomon than the figure reconstructed by modern scholarship, an ambiguous figure who cannot be judged clearly as a good king or a bad one, or as one who has attributes of both. In reference to 1 Kings 11 in particular, it also makes it much more difficult to duck one of this episode's most disturbing implications for anyone with her or his own ambitions to be wise: if even the wisest man in the world failed to grasp the most essential truths, if he ended his life worse off than he was before his wisdom, perhaps our own pursuit of ultimate understanding is also a pointless or self-destructive quest.

Since this more colorful Solomon has had much more of an influence on the world than the flatly black or white Solomons reconstructed by secular scholars—and frankly, he is more interesting as well—let us make him our focus. How could Solomon of all people go astray after false gods? What happened to his wisdom? His pious devotion to God? Premodern interpretation gives us some options to work with.

One approach was to shift the blame to Solomon's wives. Since the Bible tells us so little about these women, interpreters were free to provide them with all kinds of identities and characters. Some were remembered as beautiful and faithful—Naamah, the mother of Rehoboam, is one example; some interpreters understand her as a Ruth-like figure, a sincere convert to Solomon's religion—but others were thought to be motivated by considerations other than piety. As Moses Maimonides would later explain in his *Mishneh Torah* ("Laws of Forbidden Intercourse" 13:14–16), what drew them to Solomon's faith was not belief in God but the power and prosperity of Solomon's court. According to other interpreters, Solomon's wives were not merely insincere, they were actively deceptive, using their relationship with Solomon to convert him to idolatry.

We have already mentioned one such figure—the Queen of Sheba, whom interpretive tradition made into the thousand-and-first of Solomon's lovers and a demonic, destructive influence—but she was not alone. Another wife thought to play a catalytic role in his downfall was the daughter of Pharaoh, the first woman that Solomon marries and the one wife singled out by biblical narrative as being special in some way. In Rabbinic tradition, she is sometimes known as Bithiya or Bathiya, the same name given to the Egyptian princess that adopted Moses, but in contrast to that Bithiya, her influence on Solomon is very negative. According to the rabbis, in fact, it was on the very day that Solomon married her that the city of Rome was created, thus laying the groundwork for the terrible suffering that the Romans would later impose upon the Jews. Pharaoh's daughter was a beautiful woman, but she was also an idolater according to the rabbis, and she did everything she could to tempt the king into worshiping her gods, including using her wedding night to try to lead the king astray.

Solomon was normally a teetotaler and had abstained for the seven years during which he built the Temple, but that night was especially joyous. Not only was it their marriage night, but it was on that very day that the Temple had been finished, and so he allowed himself to drink a little too much. It was while the king was sleeping things off that the daughter of Pharaoh made an attempt to estrange him from God. Over the king's bed was a canopy, and while he was sleeping she arranged for it to be decorated with gems that sparkled like stars, not as a gift but as a trick, for when he began to stir in the morning and looked up, it appeared to him as if it was the middle of the night and that he could go back to sleep. The problem this posed is that the keys to the Temple were under his pillow. There was no access to it without them; his servants were afraid to wake the king and Solomon thus ended up sleeping so late that the priests were unable to unlock the Temple gates in time for the morning sacrifice, the first sacrifice to be offered in the Temple. That it wasn't performed on schedule was a terrible start for its cult. For some reason, Bathsheba decided that now was the time to inject some belated maternal advice, appearing to warn her son against excessive drinking (Solomon honored her words by recording them in Proverbs 31:4

—"It is not for kings to drink wine"—but I have to think that, together with a hangover, they had to be somewhat annoying). The damage was already done, however, for it was at that moment that God decided to destroy the Temple, making the whole experience the worst morning of Solomon's life and the beginning of the end of everything he had accomplished (for the sources of this tradition, which goes back to midrashic collections like *Leviticus Rabbah*, see Ginzberg's *Legends of the Jews*, volume 6, page 281, notes 13–15).

Yet another tradition focused on Abishag the Shunnamite, the beautiful virgin that Solomon's brother Adonijah had hoped to marry. We never hear of her again after 1 Kings 2, and there is no indication that she was one of Solomon's wives, but they develop a romantic relationship in postbiblical lore thanks to the Song of Songs. Though attributed to Solomon, the song actually records several voices, including a female lover—the mysterious woman who describes herself in Song of Songs 1:5 as "black and beautiful." Who was this woman? Biblical exegetes have identified her as the Queen of Sheba, the daughter of Pharaoh, and Naamah, the mother of Rehoboam. What recommends Abishag as a possibility is not only her exceptional beauty, but the title that she is given in 1 Kings: Shunnamite, which is very similar to a puzzling word used to describe the female lover in the Song of Songs 6:13: Shullamite. On this basis, it was supposed that Solomon had fallen in love with Abishag; some even suspect that his desire to marry Abishag is the real reason that Solomon had his brother Adonijah killed.

In many traditions, we should point out, Abishag is a heroic figure—a symbol of wisdom, a poetess, a witty feminist—but she can also be remembered in a negative way, as in Robert Frost's poem "Provide, Provide": "The witch that came (the withered hag) . . . was once the beauty Abishag." The *Testament of Solomon*, the supposed last words of the king, seems to reflect this negative view; it does not mention Abishag directly but it seems to have her in mind when it refers to a "Shunnamite" woman that seduces Solomon into sin. The Shunnamite in this account is a beautiful Jebusite woman whom Solomon falls deeply in love with, but her priests refuse to let them marry unless the king offers a sacrifice to their gods. Solomon refuses at first, but they insist—as does his desire for her—and so he attempts a compromise, sacrificing locusts to their god in the hope that God will not take notice of such a tiny, bloodless offering. The ruse doesn't work, however: God punishes Solomon by making him into a fool, and it is his lack of wisdom that leads him into the more egregious acts of idolatry recorded in 1 Kings 11.

According to such traditions, what undoes Solomon in the end is Eros, sexual passion, abetted in the case of Pharaoh's daughter by alcohol. However wise a sage might be, his mind was embedded in a body that generated powerful physical sensations, and these could overcome the restraints imposed by wisdom. As the philosopher Plato observes in his dialogue *Protagoras,* many people believe that the intellect is not really in charge of a person's behavior, which is more often governed by emotions and passions—pleasure, pain, love, and fear—that can push knowledge around like a slave. This is what happens to Solomon in these stories; his wisdom is matchless, and yet it is no match for the power of his desire—symbolized by his wives—which easily gets the better of it.

But according to Plato and other philosophers, a wise man could assert control over his passions, keep them in check, and if anyone should have been able to do so, it was Solomon. He himself knew full well the effects that a beautiful woman could have on a man, which is why he warns his disciples to avoid seductive women: "Do not let your heart turn aside to her ways; do not wander onto her paths, for many are those she has brought low" (Proverbs 7:25–26). Why didn't the king follow his own advice? Blaming his wives for Solomon's sin doesn't really solve the problem of how such a wise figure could behave so foolishly because, as powerful as sexual desire and alcohol can be, a sage like Solomon should have known of their danger and been able to counteract them, avoiding situations that might leave him vulnerable to their stupefying effects.

For this reason, I prefer another approach to Solomon's sin, one that does not try to explain how Solomon's wisdom failed but sees that wisdom as the problem in its own right. Of course, such a reading seems counterintuitive. The king's wisdom comes from God, and it has beneficial effects, helping the king establish justice, order, and peace; inspiring literary works of profound insight and beauty; and giving him the knowledge to heal disease and the architectural skill to build a bridge between heaven and earth. As we have also noted, however, there is something illicit and dangerous hidden in wisdom as well, and some interpreters believe that it was Solomon's wisdom, ironically, that led him astray.

The history of biblical interpretation furnishes many variations of this idea, but my personal favorite appears in the Babylonian Talmud, a tradition that blames Solomon's downfall on his exceptional knowledge of the Torah. More specifically, what gets Solomon in trouble according to this reading is his astute understanding of Deuteronomy 17, the very law that forbids him from marrying too many wives.

The inspiration for this reading is something unusual about this prohibition. Most of God's commands in the Torah are never explained—do this or don't do that, without any rationale. The behavior being enjoined might seem strange or motiveless—why can't an Israelite eat pork or light a fire on Shabbat—yet God rarely reveals why he is giving the command. One follows it without understanding its reason because it is God who is giving the order. Deuteronomy 17 is an exception, however, in that it actually explains why God is imposing a particular prohibition: the king must not acquire many wives for himself *"or else his heart will turn away."* In contrast to most of its laws, the Torah here reveals the larger purpose that God is trying to achieve by restricting a certain kind of behavior: to prevent the king from committing the much more serious offense of idolatry.

Now, as a master biblical interpreter, Solomon knew this about Deuteronomy 17, and one might think that such knowledge would have given him all the more incentive to follow it, but paradoxically it has the opposite effect, for the king reasoned that since he knew what the larger purpose of the Torah was in this instance—and since he also knew better than to worship other gods—he could skip the part about not marrying a lot of woman and just focus on the end-goal: avoiding idolatry. In retrospect this was a clear mistake, which is why, according to the Talmud, the Torah does not disclose the reasons for most of its commandments: Solomon's unhappy end illustrates that it is actually possible to understand too much about those commandments for one's own good (*Sanhedrin* 21b).

According to this interpretation, Solomon falls into sin not because he forgot what his wisdom taught him or because his intellect was overcome by some emotion or passion; his wisdom is itself the cause of his sinfulness. How so? By revealing the secrets of life, wisdom removes the barriers that ordinarily confine human ambition. This is why Solomon is able to accomplish things at such an immense scale of thousands and tens of thousands. This is why he can build a house that can accommodate a deity of immeasurable dimensions, and why he is sometimes able to operate outside the confines of God's commands. In Deuteronomy 17, for example—the same chapter that tries to restrict the number of women a king can marry— God provides clear instructions for what to do when a case is simply too baffling to solve—go to the sanctuary and let the priests decide. When faced with such a case, however, Solomon doesn't follow these instructions because he believes he doesn't have to; thanks to his wisdom, there are no baffling cases. Knowing what God knows, he simply is not constrained in the same way ordinary mortals are. But humans, the Bible contends, need limits. If nothing is hidden from them, if no secret or power is beyond their reach, they go too far, and this proves true even of Solomon, who knows so much that he thinks, falsely, that he can bypass the restrictions imposed on the rest of Israel.

In the end, of course, we are trying to solve a problem in the biblical account of Solomon's life that cannot be solved. There is no way to know what was going on in the king's mind, whether it was lust, alcohol, or wisdom that led him astray. It is conceivable that he thought he was in compliance with the law in Deuteronomy 17, which never actually specifies how many wives are too many for a king (David assumed the number was eighteen, or at least that's the excuse he gives to Abishag to justify why he never marries her, but Deuteronomy never specifies a number). It is also conceivable, given that Solomon was an old man by this point, that he had grown senile and had forgotten the law, as the first century Josephus proposed. The Bible simply does not disclose enough information to allow us to know one way or the other, and there are thus as many possible explanations for his behavior in 1 Kings 11 as Solomon had wives, perhaps even more.

But for me there is something that stands out about the Talmud's effort to connect Solomon's sin to how he interpreted the Torah. Maybe it is because this tradition reveals a connection between Solomon's story and the act of reading the Bible itself. Throughout this book, we have had to face again and again how little we can know of the Bible, stumbling over gaps that cannot be filled in, facts that cannot be verified, ambiguities that can never be resolved; and like the many generations of readers that have preceded us—the exegetes, magicians, scientists, jurists, explorers, architects, and archaeologists who have tried to solve the many questions posed by Solomon's life—we too have been unable to simply accept that the knowledge we seek is impossible. The Talmud exposes something Solomonic in this interpretive effort to reach into the Bible's hidden underside, but Solomonic not in the sense of discernment or problem-solving skill but as intellectual overreaching, a striving for secrets that we were never meant to penetrate.

And, according to some, if we knew better we would learn from Solomon's example and stop our investigation into his life right here, at the point that the biblical narrative in 1 Kings 1–11 leaves off. For a number of premodern interpretive authorities, including the author of this Talmudic story, what Solomon's sinfulness demonstrates is the folly of curiosity, of wanting to discern the hidden aspects of reality. Whatever it is that Solomon understood about the world or God or the biblical text did nothing to save the king from going astray; it might even be what got him into trouble by removing the limits that normally constrain where the mind can go. The wise should therefore learn from his mistakes to restrain not only their promiscuous sexual desires but their intellectual lust as well, the "adultery of the soul," as one source puts it. To remain faithful to God is to limit one's understanding of the world to what God has chosen to reveal through the Torah and to refrain from inquiring into those parts that God has kept hidden.

If we had followed that approach in this book, however, we would not have had much of a story to tell. The Bible's descriptions of Solomon leave one very dissatisfied, recording a loosely connected series of episodes focused mostly on the king's public career, revealing very little about his inner life or the content of his wisdom or how it was that he went astray, and raising all kinds of questions that it never addresses. What allows for the kind of depth that so many readers have detected in the biblical account—what makes it possible, for example, to explain the king's sinfulness—is the reader's Solomon-like power to see beyond the surface, to penetrate hidden motives that shouldn't be accessible to any human, to answer questions about the text that shouldn't be answerable.

The dilemma that this brings us to—Solomon's story warns against trying to know more about the Bible than it wants to reveal and yet that is what we must do to understand the Bible—is not one that we can resolve, but it is worth thinking about. What happens to Solomon in the end illustrates—depending on what one is willing to read into the story—that such curiosity can go wildly astray. This is one of the great lessons of the king's story according to Christian and Jewish tradition: the desire to know hidden things, including the desire to know the hidden implications of the Bible, is to no avail or even self-destructive. And yet knowing this cannot completely extinguish curiosity, which tends only to intensify when it discovers that the object of its desire is off-limits. Even those who blamed Solomon's sin on an illicit lust for knowledge, or on having acquired too much knowledge, could not resist the temptation of pursuing certain secrets themselves, presuming to understand more about his sin than the biblical text reveals.

How to overcome this impasse? As it happens, the story of Solomon's life offers several possible options, though to explore these options we need, once again, to go beyond the limits of the biblical text. The account of his life in 1 Kings ends with its description of his sins, briefly noting that he ruled for a total of forty years but saying nothing more about his life other than that he died and was buried in Jerusalem. If we too stopped the story there, we would have no way to address the central contradiction of Solomon's life, the way it both encourages the pursuit of wisdom and yet warns against such a quest. Fortunately, the Bible's silence has never deterred those who would understand its secrets, and some, we shouldn't be surprised to learn, have found opportunities between the lines of the biblical text to expand on the end of the king's story, developing the idea that after his sin he reached what can be considered an alternative kind of wisdom, an understanding that went beyond what God had revealed to him earlier in his life. We turn now to these interpretations not only as a way to draw our biography of Solomon to some kind of conclusion, but also to see if there might be some other conclusion to our own quest for ultimate insight other than merely to accept the little that has been revealed to us.

11

Afterthoughts

And how dieth the wise? As the fool.
—Ecclesiastes 2:16 (King James Version)

THIS BOOK HAS BEEN HARSH in its judgment of King Solomon but no harsher than the book of Kings. From the perspective of Kings, the sin that Solomon commits is nothing less than a disaster. God had promised David that his descendants would rule as an eternal dynasty, and since God does not like to break his promises, he could not simply give up on David's line, but neither could he accept Solomon's disloyalty, and so he responds with a compromise between punishment and fidelity, stripping most of the kingdom away from Solomon's successors—ten of the twelve tribes—but leaving them a small kingdom to rule from Jerusalem. But God's attempt to salvage things only postpones the end, for those who succeed Solomon as king imitate his worst traits, not his best. The kingdom formed by the rebellious ten tribes, known as the kingdom of Israel, is destroyed by the Assyrian Empire after Jeroboam and his successors fall into idolatry themselves. Judah, the remnant of Solomon's kingdom in southern Canaan, survives the Assyrian attack, but only to commit its own sins and to be decimated in turn by the Babylonians. By 586 B.C.E., there is virtually nothing left of Solomon's kingdom: the king and his sons have been executed, much of the population is deported, Jerusalem is left a desolate ruin, and all that remains of the king's great Temple are some of its furnishings and cult implements—bowls, shovels, dishes—carried off by the Babylonians as loot.

One can make a case that even now, three thousand years later, we are still living in the aftermath of Solomon's failure. His kingdom marks a turning point in history according to the Bible. Before his reign, everything that happens to Israel unfolds according to a divine plan—the Exodus from Egypt, the establishment of the monarchy, the building of the Temple. After Solomon's sin, this plan seems to break down: the Temple is destroyed, the king is displaced, the people suffer the reverse Exodus of the Exile. Religious Jews—and millions of Christians, for that matter—believe that God will someday get things back on track by sending a descendant of David, the messiah, who will do many of the same things that Solomon did—rebuild the Temple, make peace, establish justice—but this future king won't simply be picking up where Solomon left off; he will first have to undo the damage that Solomon's reign left in its wake.

But all this is to move well beyond the life of Solomon. What became of the king himself after his sin? Kings has little to say about Solomon after he goes astray, noting only that he died and was buried in the City of David with his ancestors, and it would be easy to conclude from its silence that there was nothing more to say. Without God's support, after all, the king would have lost the wisdom and power that made it possible for him to accomplish so much. At the very end of the account in

Kings, however, there is one hint that there might be more to Solomon's story than is being reported: "Now the rest of the acts of Solomon, all that he did as well as his wisdom, are they not written in the book of Acts of Solomon?" (1 Kings 11:41). What does the text mean by "the rest of the acts of Solomon"? Is there something that Kings isn't telling us about his final days? Secular scholarship cannot answer these questions, but other kinds of biblical interpretation have filled in the gap, proposing not one but several possible endings to Solomon's life for us to consider.

As it happens, in fact, the question of what happened to Solomon in the end was one of the most sharply debated aspects of his life in premodern times. One view is that he ended his life as a sinner and thus—as Catholic theology taught—went to hell, and that is where many theologians placed him. Others were not so ready to give up on Solomon, arguing that he had made it to Heaven, and what got him there, they contended, was a late-in-life act of repentance, a change of heart that moved God to forgive him. In that great epic of Catholic theology, Dante's *Divine Comedy*, the slightest and most belated act of contrition could save a sinner from eternal damnation; even a few words of contrition whispered at the moment of death could suffice, provided that the sinner repented of his sins before death. Some believed that Solomon reached such a point—including Dante, incidentally, who places Solomon in heaven. Perhaps the king repented of his sins only in his heart, in ways that are not directly registered in the biblical text, but he did so in time to secure divine forgiveness and redeem him from his many sins.

There were impressive religious authorities on both sides of this debate, and strong arguments in favor of their respective positions. Kings nowhere records an act of repentance and suggests, in fact, that Solomon remained an idolater until the end of his life (the shrines that he built lasted well beyond Solomon's death, so clearly he himself never tore them down). On the other hand, interpreters struggled to understand how a figure like Solomon could not have repented of his sins. When David acknowledged his wrongdoing—adultery and murder— God was ready to forgive him. Why wouldn't God have done the same for Solomon? And how could the wise Solomon not have eventually seen the error of his ways? It was he who built the Temple, after all—an institution whose very purpose was to allow people a way to repent of their sins and seek God's forgiveness. How could the one who opened up the gates of redemption for so many others not have recognized the possibility for redemption in his own life?

With good arguments on either side of the issue, some interpreters were simply unable to reach a definitive conclusion about Solomon's ultimate fate, and they depict Solomon in ways that convey their ambivalence. Consider, for example, the portrait of Solomon that appears in the image of the fourteenth century fresco *The Triumph of Saint Thomas Aquinas* by Andrea da Firenze (now in the Spanish chapel of the church of Santa Maria Novella in Florence). Solomon is not the large seated figure—that is Saint Thomas Aquinas—but the figure at the far right end of the line, holding open a book. The king's inclusion in the same row as other saints would seem to indicate that he too has achieved redemption, but notice one attribute of his appearance that distinguishes him from the others in the row: he alone lacks a halo! The artist reveres Solomon for his wisdom— the book that Solomon is holding open is the book of Proverbs —but he also knows that he sinned, and the absence of a halo reflects his uncertainty about the king's ultimate fate. And this artist was not alone in his ambivalence; some of the world's foremost authorities on salvation, figures like Augustine, cannot be pinned down on whether Solomon was saved or damned.

Nevertheless, a number of scholars did think it possible to determine the king's ultimate fate, and the view that interests

Andrea da Firenze, *The Triumph of St. Thomas Aquinas.* Solomon is shown to the far right of the figure on the throne. (Reproduced with permission from Art Resource)

us here, the one that finds something to salvage at the end of Solomon's life, is that he did achieve redemption by repenting his sin. There is textual support for such a possibility. While 1 Kings never mentions any kind of repentance, interpreters did find allusions to such an act in the other biblical books attributed to Solomon, in verses like Proverbs 30:2, for example: "Surely I am more foolish than anyone . . ."; or Ecclesiastes 2:11, "I turned to reflect on all the deeds that my hands had done, and all the effort I expended in doing it, and realized that it was all vanity, a chasing after the wind." Interpreters of these verses wondered how and when Solomon could have said such things. What could have led such a wise man to think himself a fool? How could he look back on his accomplishments and see them as empty and pointless? Reading these verses as expressions of contrition—Solomon's acknowledgment of his sins—not only serves to fit these sayings into his story, it provides scriptural support for those who wanted to give Solomon a second chance.

Of course, as has been true of every aspect of Solomon's life—his wisdom, the Temple, his relationship with the Queen of Sheba—the circumstances of Solomon's repentance have been imagined in different ways by different kinds of interpreters. In the thirty-eighth sura of the Quran, the king is struck with remorse as he surveys all the horses that he owns and suddenly realizes that his love of material things has displaced his love of God. In medieval Catholic tradition, the king sees the error of his ways only after he is dragged through the streets of Jerusalem and beaten with rods (this tradition may have been inspired by a real-life incident in 1077 in which a contrite Henry IV, ruler of the Holy Roman Empire, stood for three days in the snow to earn the Pope's forgiveness). My favorite example from Jewish tradition, called to my attention by my colleague Shaul Magid, comes from Nathan of Gaza, the prophetic supporter of the failed messiah Sabbatai Zvi, who draws on his belief in the transmigration of souls to educe evidence that Solomon found a way to repent after his death. Nathan recalls the story of a rabbinic sage named Rabbi Tarfon, whom Jewish legend credits with marrying three hundred women during a time of drought so as to provide them with sustenance (a story that derives from *Tosefta Ketubot* 5:1). Nathan suggests that Rabbi Tarfon was Solomon reincarnated, seeking to atone for his sin of marrying too many women by replicating the act of polygamy in a way that would do good in the world.

As different as all these traditions are, what they share is the idea that 1 Kings 11 isn't the end of Solomon's story. Something happens to him, some painful experience not recorded in

1 Kings but hinted at in other Solomonic books that makes him look back on his life and realize his mistakes. This happy ending raises its own host of questions, though: What was Solomon like in this postrepentance period? Was he changed in any way? One wants to believe that what he went through in this period made him wiser, but the wisdom he had possessed before his sin had supposedly already revealed to him every secret that it was possible for a mortal to grasp. What could Solomon have learned at the end of his life that he didn't know before?

I have to confess that I have an ulterior motive for asking such questions. Our search to understand King Solomon has mirrored the story of his life in a number of ways. Like our subject, we have presumed to know things which are impossible to know, sought to distinguish between true and false accounts where there is no clear difference between them in the absence of clear evidence, and tried to answer unsolvable riddles. We have had to confront the shortcomings of what passes for wisdom and the limited knowledge of both religious and intellectual authorities, and we have no doubt committed our own share of trespasses. Must our quest lead nowhere, then? Suggestions that Solomon's life story continued beyond the biblical account of his sins point to other possible endings. Over the ages, chastened seekers after wisdom have looked to the postwisdom phase of Solomon's life to learn whether there is anything more to learn after one realizes that understanding does not make one a better person, and might even lead one astray. What they imagined the king discovering, admittedly a projection of their own intellectual struggles, may not satisfy us as a likely or plausible ending to Solomon's story, but it at least offers some options for those who wonder what one can strive for when ultimate insight no longer seems possible or worth the trouble that comes with it.

To fill in the final moments in Solomon's life, interpreters turned once again to the three books that he had written—the

Song of Songs, Proverbs, and Ecclesiastes. Some believed that he composed these works all at once, but others noticed that there were important differences in the books' tone and perspective, and explained those differences biographically, by claiming that he wrote them at different stages in his life and that they reflect different phases in his intellectual and spiritual development. One was thought to have been written during his youth, expressing a view that is somewhat immature. The second is the work of midlife, reflecting Solomon's thinking when he was at the height of his powers. The third was written at the end of his life, recording his final insights. If we follow this tradition, it is the last of these books that is of relevance to us here and that can tell us what it is that the king came to understand at the very end of his life.

But which book is which? Which did he write first, and which was last? Interpreters answered this question in different ways. Most agreed that Proverbs reflects the midpoint of Solomon's life. Its author seems at the top of his game; he is contented, confident, wealthy, and happily married. He is thinking about the future, focused on raising his sons well, but aging and death don't overly concern him. The other two books are another matter: interpreters differed on which of Ecclesiastes and the Song of Songs was the product of his youth and that of his old age, and this difference has implications for how one imagines the final chapter of Solomon's life and what it is that he came to understand in his last days.

The more obvious of the two possible interpretations is to read the Song of Songs as the expression of Solomon's youth and Ecclesiastes as the reflections of old age. The lovers of the Song of Songs seem adolescent, after all; they are passionate and intensely physical, running around in search of the other and staying up late at night. The speaker of Ecclesiastes, on the other hand, has experienced all that life has to offer—pleasure, wealth, accomplishment—and is now overcome by thoughts of death. This interpretation seems to go back to late antiquity, reflected in rabbinic works like *Song of Songs Rabbah*, in which Rabbi Jonathan compares the Song of Songs to the bawdy songs that young men sing, and Ecclesiastes with the sententiousness of old age. This view is reflected in many artistic depictions of Solomon as well. As the lover of the Song of Songs, he often appears as a young groom; as the author of Ecclesiastes, he is weary and old.

If we follow this tradition and read Ecclesiastes as Solomon's last words, what insight does it give us into his final reflections? We find a king who is still reflective but who has learned from his life that ultimate wisdom, true understanding of life's deepest questions, is impossible, having spent his life in pursuit of knowledge only to discover that he doesn't really understand the world at all: "When I set my mind to know wisdom . . . I saw all the work of God, that no one can find out what is happening under the sun. However much effort is expended in the search, a man will not find it out; even the wise man who claims to know, he cannot find it out" (Ecclesiastes 8:16–17). Other passages in Ecclesiastes suggest that the conclusion that the king reaches in the end is to reject everything that he once sought—wealth, power, and even wisdom, which is all really just a delusion or a lie. There is nothing to learn from experience, nothing to gain from trying to understand the world, except the recognition that everything is pointless.

If this is the conclusion reached by Solomon, who knew everything there was to know, why should the rest of us persist in pursuing wisdom? That is a question that many readers of Ecclesiastes have asked, and often the answer they reach is that the search for ultimate understanding isn't worth it in the end and should be abandoned. In the early centuries of modernity, as some like Columbus, Bacon, and Newton were trying to discover the secrets that Solomon knew, others were invoking Ecclesiastes as an argument against such pursuits, Solomon's way

of warning us that, in the words of one sixteenth century the-
ologian, humans "cannot attain to the ful & absolute knowledge of things." To this day, Ecclesiastes symbolizes the mind
that has reached the end of its quest, exhausting what is possible to learn, resigning itself to permanent uncertainty. Not
only is ultimate understanding virtually impossible according
to the Solomon of this book, but the little understanding that
one can achieve only makes life more unbearable: "Those who
increase knowledge increase sorrow" (2:18). The only proper
reaction to Solomon's life according to this view of it—the lesson that the king himself drew—is to renounce one's curiosity
about the world.

This is a rather dispiriting end that calls the entirety of Solomon's life into question, and our own quest for understanding
as well, but we only need reach this conclusion if we read Ecclesiastes as Solomon's last words, and that isn't our only interpretive option; the other possibility, that he wrote Song of Songs
last, also has arguments in its favor. In a marginal comment to
the Talmudic discussion in *Baba Batra* 14b about whether Solomon's writings should be included in the Bible, Rashi records
an alternative ordering of the three books, implying a different
understanding of the king's final insights: "It seems to me that
Solomon wrote Ecclesiastes when he was young, and the Song
of Songs in his old age." Rashi does not state the reasons for
this conclusion, but I cannot help thinking that it is rooted in a
more realistic understanding of adolescence and old age than
the stereotyped images of the one as vibrant and passionate, the
other as exhausted and despairing. Who, after all, is more
likely to obsess over the pointlessness of life, who more likely
to profess a seen-it-all skepticism—a senior citizen or a teen-
ager? At least some interpreters have read Ecclesiastes as the
musings of callow youth—the medieval Jewish philosopher
Gersonides, for example, who recognized in Ecclesiastes the
skepticism of an immature mind and concluded that the young

king must have written it before God instilled him with wisdom in 1 Kings 3. If we are willing to give up our stereotypes of old age in the same way, the singer of the Song of Songs can just as plausibly be understood as an old man who still dreams of love. Death looms for this old lover, but rather than depressing him, it seems only to quicken his passion.

Reversing the books' order in this way allows for a very different ending to Solomon's story. The Solomon of the Song hasn't given up; he is still searching, but it is not wisdom he is striving for now—he has left Ecclesiastes and Proverbs behind him—but some other experience that surpasses even the divine insight that he possessed before.

And what is that experience? It is very difficult to say because, in contrast to Solomon's other writings, the song is not cast as a teaching; it does not have a lesson that can be summarized or paraphrased, and no text in the Hebrew Bible has proven harder to unlock. Ancient readers of the song believed that it registered a spiritual breakthrough possible only for one who dwells on the edges of this world, a glimpse of the heavenly realms or of God himself. In the twentieth century, the Jewish philosopher Franz Rosenzweig (who never addressed the question of when Solomon wrote the song but once suggested that a man is capable of the insight that it discloses only at "the Faustian old age of a hundred") read it as a disclosure of a truth beyond the reach of scholarship, a truth that can be described only in the language of love because it emerges solely through an ongoing, direct encounter with a Significant Other rather than disclosing itself to the mind as some fact or thesis about the world that can be analyzed or explained. These two readings of the Song of Songs—as an ancient mystical vision of God or a rejection of rationalism—are very different, but what they share is their effort to find in its lyricism some ultimate insight beyond both the wisdom of Proverbs and its view of the world as fully masterable, but also beyond the skepticism of Ec-clesiastes and its renunciation of the quest for understanding.

As we come to the end of Solomon's story then, we are faced with two possibilities: either the king came to reject his desire for knowledge or else he found a way to transcend it. There are arguments in favor of either reading, and each is also unsatisfactory. Our own struggles in this book, our inability to establish any real facts about Solomon, the irresolvable ambi-guities of the biblical text, the elusiveness of any ultimate in-sight into his character or wisdom—all seem to bear out Eccle-siastes as the last word both for the king and for us—the quest after knowledge seems only to increase frustration and uncer-tainty—but I nonetheless find myself resisting that conclusion. Curiosity—the lust to know—comes from somewhere deep in our being—if we believe Freud, it comes from the same place that generates the lust for life—and renouncing it altogether seems as potentially self-destructive as unleashing it to go wher-ever it wants.

As appealing as the Song of Songs is as the last word on wisdom, however, it is also a problematic ending to the king's story. Its Solomon is inspiring, never giving up as he does in Ecclesiastes, and penetrating deeper into the mystery of things than he ever did in his glory days as the wisest man in the world, but in the process he leaves the rest of us behind. We are told by the experts—the visionaries and the philosophers—that what the song conveys is something more than wisdom, some-thing that bears a resemblance to love if not love itself, but it remains always elusive, hinted at poetically, allegorically, but never described or explained clearly as if there was something about it that cannot be translated into the language of rational thought. Maimonides believed that the Solomon of the Song has been prohibited from sharing his insights with others—this is what the philosopher understood to be the meaning of Song of Songs 4:11: "Honey and milk are under your tongue," or, to paraphrase, "Solomon, keep the ultimate insights that you have learned to yourself." I am not sure if he was aware of Maimonides' reading, but Rosenzweig too believed that the insights of the song were incommunicable to others; in his view, the only lesson of the song that can be distilled into language is that "love is as strong as death"—the rest can only be hinted at through allusive poetry, never clearly articulated as a thesis or a teaching. The Song of Songs, according to these interpretations, only lets us see the king *seek* his beloved: the insight that Solomon reaches in the end is never clearly revealed to us, lying beyond what can be understood through the power of thought.

Such reservations, among others, give one pause about accepting either Ecclesiastes or the Song of Songs as a record of Solomon's final thoughts; there are reasons to accept either one, but reasons to reject each position too, and the truth is that no amount of reasoning can help us to choose between them. If we had the kind of divine insight that Solomon possessed, we would be able to solve this problem, to make a definitive decision between skepticism and mysticism, but of course we don't, and even if it were possible to acquire such insight, what we have learned about it through our brief encounter with King Solomon and the various kinds of folly that his wisdom engendered gives us reason to be suspicious of whatever it might reveal.

This is why I have decided that the only way to end this account of Solomon's life is not with a Solomonic judgment but rather with a compromise, a split decision between Ecclesiastes and the Song of Songs that imagines the king, in his last moments, reaching a view of life that combines the perspective of both books into an outlook that is neither intellectual despair nor the superrational insight of mysticism but rather something in between or perhaps a combination of both: "Love is as strong as death." One way to understand what Solomon is saying here is: "love = death"—that is, the Song of Songs, the song of love = Ecclesiastes and its musings about death. The two books are equivalent or complementary at some level. As different as they are, after all, both lead the reader to the same insight—that the world's deepest secrets go beyond understanding. I would like to propose that the king's final act was to respond to the irresolvable mystery of life in not one but two ways that might seem contradictory at first but that can in fact coexist as part of one equation: that he came to recognize the mind's limits, how little power it has to penetrate life's secrets, but also, at the same time, that he did not give up in the face of those limits, was still willing to go into the darkness, to search late into the night, to keep knocking at the door even without anyone ever opening it.

Now I am of course not trying to describe here what Solomon was actually thinking in his final moments, any more than I have presumed to describe his life as he actually lived it. Though our reconstruction is not any more far-fetched than the other endings imagined for the king, it is in no way provable, historically plausible, or, frankly, even possible—remember that there is little chance that either Ecclesiastes or the Song of Songs was actually written by the king, much less that he wrote them at the same time. There is, however, a reason to take it seriously. Those searching for ultimate insight often find themselves stuck somewhere between the experiences registered by Ecclesiastes and the Song of Songs—we resign ourselves to not understanding even as we yearn to understand, vacillating back and forth—and I at least have a hard time detecting progression in the movement from one state to the other, growing older but no more able today to decide in favor of one book's view or the other than I was ten or twenty years ago. The last moments of Solomon as imagined here suggest life may always remain so, that this mixture of resignation and restless searching, not absolute understanding, is where the search for wisdom leads to in the end—a conclusion that rings true even if it isn't true for the king in a historical sense. In other words, the Solomon we have been describing here—here and throughout this biography, for that matter—isn't a historical figure but he is a recognizably human one, and what makes his life real is the way that it mirrors our own strivings and doubts.

FOR THOSE SEEKING TO KNOW MORE

Beyond retelling Solomon's story, this book seeks to introduce readers to Solomon's role in the history of humanity's pursuit of inaccessible wisdom, to how his story has shaped, and been shaped by, religion, philosophy, magic, literature, art, architecture, science, exploration, and other ways in which humans seek to understand hidden and inaccessible aspects of life. Most of the following bibliography is for general readers interested in learning more about this interpretive history, but a few studies are more specialized and I mention them to acknowledge the ideas and information I have taken from them. For additional bibliography—and for another approach to telling the story of King Solomon—see Walter Bruggemann's *Solomon: Israel's Ironic Icon of Human Achievement* (Westminster: John Knox Press, 2003).

Preface

Pre-modern interpretations of Solomon's story are found in innumerable Jewish, Christian, and Muslim sources. No single study reviews them all, but three resources can give you a sense of some of the better-known interpretive expansions of his story in Jewish and Christian tradition. Louis Ginzberg's *Legends of the Jews* (Philadelphia: Jewish Publication Society, 1968), comprises seven volumes; four are a paraphrase of the Bible from Adam to Esther in light of early Jewish interpretive tradition, while the remaining three consist of detailed footnotes that will lead you to the original sources from which these traditions come. Some of these same legends are retold by the Hebrew poet Haym Bialik in *And It Came to Pass: Legends and Stories About King David and King Solomon* (ed. Herbert Danby, New York: Hebrew Pub. Co., 1938). For another sampling of Jewish, Christian, and Muslim Solomonic legends, see John Seymour's antiquated but still engaging *Tales of King Solomon* (London: Oxford University, 1924), which has recently been reprinted by Kessinger Publishing.

Moving from premodern interpretation to modern scholarship, one can plunge into current research on the historical Solomon by reading the essays in Lowell Handy (ed.), *The Age of Solomon: Scholarship at the Turn of the Millennium* (Leiden: Brill, 1997). For the nitty-gritty on the textual discrepancies between the Masoretic and Septuagint versions of Solomon's story, see Percy S. F. Van Keulen, *Two Versions of the Solomon Narrative* (Leiden: Brill, 2005). For the debate about whether Solomon's kingdom existed, the strongest argument in favor of its historical plausibility is Amihai Mazar, "The Search for David and Solomon: An Archaeological Perspective," in Brian Schmidt (ed.), *The Quest for the Historical Israel* (Atlanta: Society of Biblical Literature, 2007), 117–39. For the argument against, Israel Finkelstein has an essay in the same volume, "King Solomon's Golden Age: History or Myth?" (107–16), and he presents his case at greater length in a book co-authored with Neil Silberman, *David and Solomon: In Search of the Bible's Sacred Kings and the Roots of the Western Tradition* (New York: Free Press, 2006).

Chapter 1: A Life in Letters

For the wordplay buried in the names of Solomon and other biblical figures, see Moshe Garsiel, *Biblical Names: A Literary Study of*

Midrashic Derivations and Puns (Ramat Gan: Bar Ilan University, 1991). My analysis of Solomon's name is especially indebted to Amos Frisch, "Derivations of Solomon's Name in the Book of Kings," *Beth Mikra* 45 (1999): 84–96 (in Hebrew).

Chapter 2: A Lust for Knowledge

To learn more about the dysfunctional family that Solomon comes from, see Stephen McKenzie, *King David: A Biography* (Oxford: Oxford University, 2000); or Baruch Halpern, *David's Secret Demons: Messiah; Murderer, Traitor, King* (Eerdmans: Grand Rapids, Michigan, 2001), which uncovers a scandal between the lines of Solomon's birth story. For a psychoanalytic reading of the Bible, see Avivah Gottleib Zornberg, *The Murmuring Deep: Reflections on the Biblical Unconscious* (New York: Schocken, 2009). For more on curiosity and its association with lust, see Roger Shattuck, *Forbidden Knowledge: From Prometheus to Pornography* (New York: St. Martin's, 1996), which recounts the history of humanity's lust for knowledge, from Eve to the present, though it overlooks Solomon.

Chapter 3: Succession Struggles

Many biblical scholars read the story of Solomon's succession in 1 Kings 1–2 as a work of court propaganda composed by a scribe living in the time of Solomon, a view that traces back to the German scholar Leonard Rost in a 1926 work published in English as *The Succession to the Throne of David* (trans. M. D. Rutter and D. M. Gunn; Sheffield: Almond, 1982). For a fictional working out of this idea, see Stefan Heym, *The King David Report* (Evanston, Illinois: Northwestern University Press, 1998). For more on what is historical and what is literary in 1 Kings 1–2, see Ron Hendel, *Remembering Abraham: Culture, Memory and History in the Hebrew Bible* (New York: Oxford University Press, 2005), 75–94. For more on Joab as a sympathetic figure in Jewish tradition, see Ephraim Urbach, "The Death of Joab: Political History in the Eyes of the Sages," reprinted in Ephraim Urbach, *Collected Writings in Jewish Studies* (Jerusalem: Hebrew University Magnes Press, 2009), 473–90.

Chapter 4: Solomonic Judgments

The question of how Solomon managed to solve the case of the two prostitutes, as straightforward as his solution might seem, has perplexed many scholars, premodern and modern alike. For a review of some of the proposed solutions, see Moshe Garsiel, "Revealing and Concealing as a Narrative Strategy in Solomon's Judgement," *Catholic Biblical Quarterly* 64 (2002): 229–47. For more on the philosophers admiring Solomon in the scene from Pompey, see Theodore Feder, "Solomon, Socrates and Aristotle," *Biblical Archaeology Review* 34, no. 5 (September–October 2008): 32–26.

The definitive history of how Solomon's wisdom has been understood over the ages is yet to be written, but for discussion of how some of the most important medieval Jewish commentators understood it, see David Berger, "The Wisest of All Men: Solomon's Wisdom in Medieval Jewish Commentaries on the Book of Kings," in Y. Elman and J. S. Gurock (eds.), *Hazon Nahum: Studies in Jewish Law, Thought and History Presented to Dr. Normal Lamm* (Hoboken, New Jersey: KTAV, 1997), 93–114. For more on the Solomonic figures of our own age, see Stephen Whitfield, "The Jew as Wisdom Figure," *Modern Judaism* 13 (1993): 1–24.

Chapter 5: Sacred Book, Satanic Verses

The three canonical writings attributed to Solomon—Proverbs, the Song of Songs, and Ecclesiastes—have each generated an immense bibliography. For introductions to Proverbs and Ecclesiastes, see James Crenshaw, *Old Testament Wisdom: An Introduction* (Atlanta: John Knox Press, 1981); and Roland Murphy, *The Tree of Life: An Exploration of Biblical Wisdom Literature* (New York: Doubleday, 1990). Murphy has also produced a good commentary on the Song of Solomon, *The Song of Songs: A Commentary on the Book of Canticles or the Song of Songs* (Minneapolis: Fortress, 1990). Most commentaries focus on the books themselves but a new series aims to survey the history of their interpretation. See Eric Christianson, *Ecclesiastes Through the Centuries* (Oxford: Blackwell, 2007); and a forthcoming volume by Francis Landy and Fiona Black, *Song of Songs Through the Centuries*. For more on the *mashal* as understood in rabbinic tradition, see David Stern, *Parables in Midrash: Narrative and Exegesis in Rabbinic Literature* (Cambridge: Harvard University Press, 1991).

While it is not a part of the Jewish or Protestant biblical canons, the *Wisdom of Solomon* is a part of Catholic and Orthodox biblical canons. See David Winston, *The Wisdom of Solomon* (Anchor Bible; Garden City, New York: Doubleday, 1979). Translations of other pseudo-Solomonic texts like the *Testament of Solomon* and the *Psalms of Solomon* appear in J. H. Charlesworth's two volume *The Old Testament Pseudepigrapha* (Garden City, New York: Doubleday, 1983–85). For other magical writings attributed to Solomon—and for a discussion of when and how he came to be perceived as a magician—see Pablo Torijano, *Solomon the Esoteric King: From King to Magus, Development of a Tradition* (Leiden: Brill, 2002). On the tradition that some of Solomon's writings were hidden, see David Halperin, "The Book of Remedies, the Canonization of Solomonic Writings, and the Riddle of Pseudo-Eusebius," *Jewish Quarterly Review* 72 (1982): 269–92. On Solomon as a source of the Faust myth, I am indebted to Michael Hattaway, "The Theology of Marlowe's Doctor Faustus," *Renaissance Drama* n.s. 3 (1970): 51–78.

Chapter 6: The King of Kings

Among the various rulers that modeled themselves on Solomon, the best-known in English tradition are Queen Elizabeth and James I (James's identification with Solomon encouraged the interest in Solomon evident in seventeenth century thinkers like Francis Bacon). What I know about their relationship to Solomon comes from William Tate, *Solomonic Iconography in Early Stuart England: Solomon's Wisdom, Solomon's Folly* (Lewiston, New York: Edwin Mellen Press, 2001). For Solomon as the ideal ruler in Jewish thought, see Abraham Melamed, *The Philosopher-King in Medieval and Renaissance Jewish Political Thought* (Albany, New York: State University of New York Press, 2003). For an example of how Solomon was used to argue against the institution of monarchy, see Jonathan Israel, "Spinoza, King Solomon, and Frederik van

Leenhof's Spinozistic Republicanism," *Studia Spinozana*, vol. 11 (1995): 303–18. The Bible both reflects and contests ideas of kingship prevalent in the ancient Near East. For a dated but still useful study of kingship in the ancient Near East and its role as a guardian of the cosmic order, see Henri Frankfurt, *Kingship and the Gods: A Study of Ancient Near Eastern Religion as the Integration of Society and Nature*, 1st ed. (Chicago: University of Chicago Press, 1948). The subtle connection between Solomon and Pharaoh is discussed by Yair Zakovitch, *"And You Shall Tell Your Son"—The Concept of the Exodus in the Bible* (Jerusalem: Magness, 1992), 92–97.

Chapter 7: Building Heaven on Earth

A beautifully illustrated and accessibly written survey of how Solomon's Temple has been seen by Jews, Christians, Muslims, Masons, and others has recently been published: William Hamblin and David Rolph Seely, *Solomon's Temple: Myth and History* (London: Thames and Hudson, 2007), which contains ample suggestions for further reading about the Temple.

Chapter 8: Mining for Solomon's Gold

The story of the search for Solomon's gold is scattered over several articles. Note, among other studies of the subject: Scott Carroll, "Solomonic Legend: The Muslims and the Great Zimbabwe," *International Journal of African Historical Studies*, vol. 21 (1988): 233–47. Jorge Magasich-Airola and Jean-Marc de Beer, *America Magica: When Renaissance Europe Thought It Had Conquered Paradise* (trans. Monica Sandor; London: Anthem, 2006), 53–67; and James Romm, "Biblical History and the Americas: The Legend of Solomon's Ophir, 1492–1591," in *The Jews and the Expansion of Europe to the West 1450–1800*, ed. Paulo Bernadini and Norman Fiering (New York and Oxford: Berghan, 2001), 27–46. *King Solomon's Mines* initiated a tradition of popular fiction that is still very much alive today. For a recent example, a work of nonfiction set in Ethiopia, see Tahir Shah, *In Search of King Solomon's Mines* (New York: Arcade, 2003). For more on the Phoenicians, including their shipping operations, a good survey is Glenn Markoe, *Phoenicians* (Berkeley, California: University of California Press, 2000).

Chapter 9: Difficult Questions from a Dubious Queen

For the Queen as imagined in Jewish, Christian, and Islamic tradition, see James Pritchard (ed.), *Solomon and Sheba* (London: Phaedon, 1974), and for further analysis, along with translations of some of the pertinent Jewish and Islamic texts, see Jacob Lassner, *Demonizing the Queen of Sheba: Boundaries of Gender and Culture in Postbiblical Judaism and Medieval Islam* (Chicago and London: University of Chicago Press, 1993). For the impact that the Queen has had on art, literature, and film, along with a review of the archaeology of the Yemenite kingdom of Saba/Sheba, see St. John Simpson, *Queen of Sheba: Treasures from Ancient Yemen* (London: Trustees of the British Museum, 2002). My understanding of the Queen's questions also owes much to Dina Stein, "A King, a Queen, and the Riddle Between: Riddles and Interpretation in a Late Midrashic Text," in *Untying the Knot: On Riddles and Other Enigmatic Modes*, ed. Galit Hasan-Rokem and David Shulman (New York and Oxford: Oxford University Press, 1996), 125–47.

Chapter 10: A Thousand and One Sex Scandals

On the women in Solomon's life, see Linda Schearing, "A Wealth of Women: Looking Behind, Within and Beyond Solomon's Story," in *The Age of Solomon: Scholarship at the Turn of the Millennium*, ed. Lowell Handy (Leiden: Brill, 1997), 428–56. I have been intrigued by David Pinsky's novel *King Solomon's Thousand Wives*, but so far as I have been able to determine with the help of my colleague Zachary Baker, it does not appear to have been published in book form, certainly not in translation. Solomon's love life, especially his supposed romance with the Queen of Sheba, has inspired more than its share of other literary works, however—a lot of cheap romance novels but also some literary gems. One can find an online sampling at a Web site devoted to the Queen of Sheba: www.isidore-of-seville.com/sheba/index.html. Others of Solomon's lovers have gotten less attention but have not been completely ignored, as two recent examples attest: the poem "A Letter Home" by the Canadian writer Yerra Sugarman, appearing in her *The Bag of Broken Glass* (Riverdale, NY: Sheep Meadow Press, 2008), views Solomon from the perspective of the daughter of Pharaoh, while one of Brazil's foremost novelists, Moacyr Scliar (whose work has been included among the greatest works of modern Jewish literature), has written a novel about another wife, *A Mulher que Escreveu a Biblia* (*The Woman Who Wrote the Bible*), though it has not been translated into English so far as I know.

Chapter 11: Afterthoughts

The subject of Solomon's repentance and afterlife could inspire an entire treatise in the Middle Ages, but now it is addressed only in specialized studies that aren't accessible to general readers but which I want to acknowledge for what I have learned from them: Michael Stone, "Concerning the Penitence of Solomon," *Journal of Theological Studies*, vol. 29 (1978): 1–19; Stewart Vanning, *Medieval Christian and Jewish Approaches to the Sins of King Solomon and His Salvation or Damnation with Special Reference to the Treatise of Philip of Harvengt* (Ph.D. diss., Bar Ilan University, 2002), and Lorenzo Di Tommaso, "Pseudepigrapha Notes III: 4. Old Testament Pseudepigrapha in the Yale University MS Collection," forthcoming in the *Journal for the Study of the Pseudepigrapha*. I thank Drs. Vanning and Di Tomasso for sharing their unpublished or forthcoming research with me.

On the question of when Solomon wrote his three books, see Seymour Feldman, "The Wisdom of Solomon: A Gersonidean Interpretation," *Gersonide en son temps* (ed. G. Dahan; Louvain: Peeters, 1991): 61–80. On Ecclesiastes as a warning against intellectual inquiry, see Michael Hattaway, "Paradoxes of Solomon: Learning in the English Renaissance," *Journal of the History of Ideas*, vol. 29 (1968): 499–530. For the reading of the Song of Songs as the record of a mystical experience, a reading perhaps introduced by Rabbi Akiba, see Joseph Dan, "The Religious Experience of the Merkavah," in *Jewish Spirituality: From the Bible*

Through the Middle Ages, ed. Arthur Green (New York: Crossroad, 1986), 289–312, esp. 294–98. Rosenzweig's reading of the Song of Songs, drafted while he lay in the bed of his lover Margrit Rosenstock, appears in *The Star of Redemption* (trans. W. Hallo; Notre Dame, Indiana: University of Notre Dame Press, 1970), 198–205. For help with understanding Rosenzweig's interpretation, I turned to Mara Benjamin, *Rosenzweig's Bible: Reinventing Scripture for Jewish Modernity* (Cambridge: Cambridge University Press, 2009); and Paul Mendes-Flohr, "Between Sensual and Heavenly Love: Franz Rosenzweig's reading of the Song of Songs," in *Scriptural Exegesis—The Shapes of Culture and Religious Imagination: Essays in Honor of Michael Fishbane*, ed. Deborah Green and Laura Lieber (Oxford: Oxford University Press, 2009), 310–18.

INDEX

Abdemon, 142

Abiathar, 35, 43, 45, 47

Abishag, 19, 39, 44–45, 160, 164

Absalom, 1–2, 8–10, 12, 16, 19, 36, 43–44

Adam, 25–26, 28–29

Adonijah, 1–2, 16, 35–38, 40–41, 44–45, 47, 160

Ahijah, 13

Alemanno, Yohanan, 60, 75, 128

Amnon, 9, 12, 16, 19

Ark of the covenant, 36, 101–2, 106

Asmodeus, 79–80, 82, 110, 128. See also Devil; Mephistopheles

Azitiwada, 90–91, 93

Bacon, Francis, 52, 70–71, 76, 78, 105, 176

Barreto, Isabel, 137

Bathsheba: affair with David, 9, 18, 149; as mother of Solomon, 4–6, 19–20, 37, 159; rebuke of Solomon, 159–60; role in Solomon's ascension, 35, 38, 40, 42, 45

Ben Sira, 146

Bilqis, 140. See also Queen of Sheba

Boaz, 4

Chronicles, x, 15, 65, 97, 113, 137; account of Solomon's lineage, 4, 16, 33; and critical biblical scholarship, xiv, xvi, xxi; description of the Temple, 100, 103, 105, 113; prophecy concerning Solomon, 7, 9–10, 12, 15

1 Chronicles: 22, 7; 22:9, 8

2 Chronicles: 3:6, 123; 8:11, 97

Columbus, Christopher, 116–18, 120, 127, 176

curiosity, xxii, xxvi, 125; danger of, 82, 165–66, 179; and sexuality, 27–28. See also knowledge; libido sciendi; wisdom daughter of Pharaoh, 29, 94, 97, 150–52, 158–61

David (King), xx, 1, 7, 10, 45, 48, 84, 164; as adulterer, 5, 149, 153, 171; City of, 94, 169; descendants of, 36–38, 41, 168–69; dynasty of 4, 18, 42; failure to build temple, 8, 11, 100; as father of Solomon, 14, 19, 21, 23, 44, 86, 152–53; last words to Solomon, 21, 23, 44

demon. *See* devil

Deuteronomistic Historian, 156

Deuteronomy, 164; *1:39*, 27; *7:3–4*, 152; *17*, 127, 129, 155, 157, 162–64; *17:15–16*, 94

Devil, 79–80, 110, 145–46. *See also* Asmodeus; Mephistopheles

Dome of the Rock, xix, 99, 107

Ecclesiastes (Qoheleth), x–xi, 72–74, 79, 129, 131, 175–81; *1:3*, 130; *1:12*, 129; *1:17*, xxiii; *2:4–8*, 129, 131; *2:11*, 172; *2:16*, 168; *2:18*, 177; *8:16–17*, 176

Eli, house of, 35

En-rogel, 36

Ethiopia, 87, 139–40, 148, 151–52; *Kebra Nagast* as national epic, 151. *See also* Queen of Sheba

Eve, 25–29, 79

Exodus: as event, 95, 101, 108–9, 157, 169; story of, 18, 25, 43, 95–96, 150

Ezion-Geber, xviii, 85, 116, 123, 126

Faust (Dr. Faustus), 80–81

Freemasons, 105–6

Freud, Sigmund, xvii, 17–18, 20, 23–28, 30–31, 52, 60, 69–70, 179

Genesis: *3:7*, 27; *29:35*, 3; *49:8–10*, 3

Gezer, 85

Gibeon, 23–24, 62

Hadad, 95

Haggard, H. Rider, 113, 118, 121–22, 125

harem, 18, 150–51

Hazor, xviii, 85

Hezekiah, 72, 78

Hiram (architect), 103, 105, 114

Hiram (Phoenician King), 11, 91, 100, 122–23, 125–26, 128, 142

Jabez, 4, 14, 21

Jacob, 3–4, 21

James I, 87. *See also* King James Bible

Jehoshaphat, 126

Jeroboam, 13, 15, 169

Jerusalem, 44–46, 62, 86, 89, 127–30, 166, 173; associations with David, 16, 19, 35–36; associations with Temple, xviii, 50, 85, 97–99, 100, 102, 107; excavations, xix, xx; link to Solomon's name, 11, 14

Jesus, 86

Joab, 35–36, 38, 41, 43, 45–47, 66; trial of, 48

Job (biblical book), 125

Jonathan, 33

Josephus, 26, 70, 116, 142, 164; interpretation of Solomon's judgment, xv, 58; references to the Queen of Sheba, 137, 140

Judah, kingdom of 3, 13, 169, son of Jacob 3–4

kingdom: of David, xx, 10; of Israel, 169; schism, 13–15, 168; of Solomon, 11–15, 84–87, 96, 107, 137, 149, 169.

King James Bible 87, 168. *See also* James I

Kings (biblical books), xx, 33, 90, 92, 97, 111; account of Queen of Sheba, 134, 137; ambiguity of, 7, 12, 16, 62, 65, 67, 113, 170; and critical biblical scholarship, xiv, xvi; descriptions of Temple, 100–103, 106, 109–10; negative portrayal of Solomon, 14–15

1 Kings, x, xxi, 35, 39, 91, 93–94, 160, 172; *1:1–4*, 39; *1–8*, 109; *1–10*, 149, 156; *1–11*, x, 2, 10, 20, 126, 157, 165; *1:11–14*, 37; *1:15*, 39; *1:17–21*, 38; *1:30–31*, 40; *1:52*, 43; *1–2*, 34,

42, 49; 2, 43, 63, 160; 2:1–9, 20; 2:2,
21; 2:6, 21; 2:9, 21, 42; 3, xv, 22–23,
29, 42–43, 49, 54, 57, 178; 3:1–2,
93–94; 3:4–15, 24; 3:5–14, 23; 3:12,
71; 3:13, 89; 3:17–22, 54; 3:24–25,
58; 3–10, 91; 4:21, 85; 5, 93, 95; 5:1,
85; 5:4, 11, 75; 5:11, 34; 5:12, 11;
5:13, 69, 76; 5:18, 75; 5:26, 11; 5–8,
98; 7:23, xii; 7:51, 11; 9:13, 125;
9:25, 11; 9:26–28, 114; 9–10, 114;
10, 30, 93; 10:3, 145; 10:7, 138; 10:8,
133; 10:12, 126; 10:20, 87; 10:22,
115; 11, 110, 149–50, 152, 154, 156,
158, 161, 164, 173; 11:1, 30; 11:1–2,
150; 11:4, 13; 11:7, 154; 11:41, 170
2 Kings, xiv, 156
"King Solomon's Dilemma," 61
knowledge, xii, 42, 77, 80, 115, 120,
147–48; dangerous, 80–82, 162–63,
166; divine, xi, 49, 63–65; forbidden
and hidden, 28, 31, 68–69, 77–79,
82, 103, 105; scientific 27, 31–32,
51–52, 70–71, 76–79, 81, 105, 155;
in Solomonic writings, xiii, xxiii, 22,
74–75, 77, 176–77; Tree of, 25,
27–28. See also curiosity; wisdom

libido sciendi, 27. See also curiosity;
knowledge
Lorenz, Konrad, 69–70, 81

magic, 31, 51, 65, 70, 75, 77, 80, 103.
See also Asmodeus; Faust; Mephis-
topheles; Solomon: magical ability;
Solomon: ring of
magic carpet, 136
Makeda, 139. See also Ethiopia; Queen
of Sheba
mashal (proverb), xxv–xxvi, 11, 73, 74
Masoretic Bible, xv–xvi, 6, 89, 95
Megiddo, xvii–xviii, xx, 85
Menelik, 139–40. See also Queen of
Sheba
Mephistopheles, 80. See also Devil;
Faust
messiah, 14, 86, 139, 169, 173
mining, 52, 124–25, 128

Moses, 18, 21, 33, 62, 84, 98, 102, 152;
and Deuteronomy, 127, 152, 156;
and Egypt, 94, 101

Naamah, 152, 158, 160
Nathan (brother of Solomon), 17
Nathan (prophet), 6–7, 9, 12, 14,
35–38, 40, 42, 44, 109–10
Nebuchadnezzar, 89, 128, 146–47
Newton, Sir Isaac, 104–5, 176

Odes of Solomon, 75
Ophir, 119–20, 122–25, 132; biblical
references, 114, 115, 126; identification with Africa, 116, 118, 120; identification with New World, 117–18

parable, xxv–xxvi, 11, 73–74, 80, 82,
86. See also mashal
Parahyba Inscription, 123
Parker, Montagu, xviii
peace, 8, 10, 13, 65, 86. See also
shalom; Solomon: as peacemaker
Pharaoh, 95–96, 150
proverb, 11, 22, 63, 65, 72–73, 83. See
also mashal; parable
Proverbs (biblical book), x, 74, 112,
146, 178; 1:7, 22; 7:18, 29; 7:22, 29;
7:25, 161; 8:27–30, 84; 11:28, 131;
15:17, 130; 22:4, 131; 30:2, 172;
31:4, 159–60
Psalms, 22, 75; 111:10, 22
Psalms of Solomon, 75

Qoheleth. See Ecclesiastes
Queen of Sheba, 29, 93, 133, 149, 151,
158, 160; excavations concerning,
121, 140–41; film representations
of, 134–35; location of homeland,
136–41, 148; riddles of, 65, 141–44,
147; sex appeal, 134, 136; significance in Ethiopia, 139–40, 148,
151–52; significance in Yemen, 136,
139–41; skepticism, 138, 145;
throne of, 144–45. See also Bilqis;
Ethiopia; Jerusalem; Makeda;
Menelik; riddle; Yemen
Quran, 136, 144, 173

Rastafarians, 139
Rehoboam, 75, 152, 158, 160
Rezin, 95
riddle, 22, 141–43, 145, 148

Samuel (biblical books), 7, 10; 1
   Samuel, 96; *8:5*, 93; 2 Samuel, 9,
   17; *5:11*, xx; 7, 7–8, 14, 110; *12*, 6;
   12:24, 5; *12:24–25*, 6; *16*, 43
Samuel (prophet), 21, 33, 92–93
Saul, 1–2, 18, 43–48, 92
Selassie, Haile, 87, 139
Septuagint, xv, 95, 118
shalom, 8, 10–11. *See also* peace
Sheba, location of, 122–24, 136–37,
   141, 148. *See also* Ethiopia; Queen
   of Sheba; Yemen
Shimei, 43–44, 46–48
Solomon: ability to talk to animals,
   31, 69–70, 72; archaeological evidence for, xvii–xviii, 55; artistic
   representations of, xvi, 55–57;
   birth, 9, 12; building activity, 11,
   65, 83–85, 98, 100, 108–10; as *cosmocrat*, 88; death and afterlife, xxiv,
   95, 170–71, 173, 175–76, 178,
   180–81; dream at Gibeon, 23–25,
   28–31, 49, 71, 127; early life of,
   19–23, 26, 28; exile of 45, 129–31;
   idolatry, xxiii, 12, 153–59, 161, 163,
   170; as king of kings, 85–86, 93;
   judgment, xvi, 48, 55–63, 66–68,
   94, 97, 138, 180; magical ability, 48,
   50, 70, 75–81; marriages of, 12–13,
   29–30, 94, 150–52, 155, 158–61,
   163–64; messianic association, 14,
   86; name of, 1–2, 4–6, 10–15; as
   peacemaker, 8–11, 13, 65, 86; and
   Queen of Sheba, 134, 138, 141,
   143–48; reason for downfall,
   161–65; repentance, 173–74; ring
   of, xix, 70, 99, 128; as ruler 48, 58,
   83–90, 92–98, 125, 151; and science, 31–32, 71, 76, 82; Solomonic
   writings, x–xi, 72, 174–81; succession, 8–12, 34–38, 40–41, 43–46;
   treatment of enemies, 43–44,

46–47, 49, 58, 65; wealth of,
   111–15, 117–21, 124–32, 137, 155.
   See also Ecclesiastes; magic,
   Proverbs; Song of Songs; Temple;
   wisdom
Solomon Islands, 118, 137
Song of Songs (Song of Solomon)
   (biblical book), x–xi, 28–29, 72–73,
   79, 149, 160, 175–76, 178–81; *1:5*,
   160; *4:11*, 179–80; *6:13*, 160
Spinoza, Baruch de, xii–xiv, xxiv, 105
"Succession Narrative," 34
Suleiman the Magnificent, 86

Tamar (sister of Solomon), 9, 49
Tarshish, 114–20, 122, 125
Temple, xviii, 50, 98–99; as architectural model, 71, 99, 107–8, 121,
   127; biblical description, xii, 91,
   100–101, 103–4, 106–7, 110–11;
   in Christian tradition, 99, 104, 107,
   110; completion, 11, 13, 79, 159;
   construction, 84–85, 98, 107–10,
   121, 151, 159, 169, 171; design,
   83–84, 103; destruction, 15, 72,
   101, 147, 160, 169; excavations of,
   xviii–xix; Holy of Holies, 100, 102;
   Islamic tradition and, 99, 107; Jewish tradition and, 105, 108, 110; as
   midpoint in biblical history,
   108–110; parallels with ancient
   Near Eastern Temples, 100, 106–7;
   repentance and, 111. *See also* Ark of
   the covenant; Jerusalem; David;
   Freemasons; Solomon; wisdom
Templo, Leon, 105
Testament of Solomon, 75, 110, 160
Throne of Solomon, 87–89, 126, 128

Uriah, 6, 36

wisdom, xii, 11, 21–23, 28, 31–32, 42,
   48–50, 53, 153; ancient versus modern conceptions, 51–53, 64, 70–71;
   association with political cunning,
   42–43, 48–49; association with sexual desire, 27–29; dark side of,

66–67, 77–79, 148, 162–65; divine versus human, 62–63, 71–72, 79, 90, 145, 157; of elderly Solomon, 174–81; Eve's desire for, 26–27; and magic, 50–51, 70, 75–81, 103; and order, 83–84, 162; proverbs as expression of, 11, 22, 65, 72–73, 83; revelation at Gibeon, 26, 29; role in creation, 84–85; and science, 31–32, 52, 70, 76, 81–82, 103–4; of young Solomon, 22–23, 26–29. *See also* curiosity; knowledge; *libido sciendi;* magic; proverb; riddle

Wisdom of Solomon, 75, 77, 85, 153

Yedidyah (alternate name for Solomon), 6, 17
Yemen, 136, 139–41. *See also* Queen of Sheba

Zadok, 87
Zornberg, Aviva, 18, 20, 25

JEWISH LIVES is a major series of interpretive
biography designed to illuminate the imprint of eminent Jewish
figures upon literature, religion, philosophy, politics, cultural and
economic life, and the arts and sciences. Subjects are paired with
authors to elicit lively, deeply informed books that explore the
breadth and complexity of Jewish experience
from antiquity through the present.

Jewish Lives is a partnership of Yale University Press
and the Leon D. Black Foundation.

Anita Shapira and Steven J. Zipperstein
are series editors.

ALSO IN THE SERIES:

Sarah: The Life of Sarah Bernhardt, by Robert Gottlieb
Moses Mendelssohn, by Shmuel Feiner

FORTHCOMING TITLES INCLUDE:

Bernard Berenson, by Rachel Cohen
Leonard Bernstein, by Allen Shawn
Louis Brandeis, by Jeffrey Rosen
Martin Buber, by Paul Mendes-Flohr
Moshe Dayan, by Mordechai Bar-On
Bob Dylan, by Ron Rosenbaum
Sigmund Freud, by Adam Phillips
George Gershwin, by Gary Giddins
Emma Goldman, by Vivian Gornick
Hank Greenberg, by Mark Kurlansky
Lillian Hellman, by Dorothy Gallagher
Vladimir Jabotinsky, by Hillel Halkin
Jacob, by Yair Zakovich
Franz Kafka, by Saul Friedlander
Abraham Isaac Kook, by Yehudah Mirsky
Rashi, by Jack Miles